INTRODUCING
ISSUES WITH
OPPOSING
VIEWPOINTS®

Immigration and Travel Restrictions

M. M. Eboch, Book Editor

GREENHAVEN
PUBLISHING

Published in 2019 by Greenhaven Publishing, LLC
353 3rd Avenue, Suite 255, New York, NY 10010

Copyright © 2019 by Greenhaven Publishing, LLC

First Edition

Articles in Greenhaven Publishing anthologies are often edited for length to meet page requirements. In addition, original titles of these works are changed to clearly present the main thesis and to explicitly indicate the author's opinion. Every effort is made to ensure that Greenhaven Publishing accurately reflects the original intent of the authors. Every effort has been made to trace the owners of the copyrighted material.

Cataloging-in-Publication Data

Names: Eboch, MM, editor.
Title: Immigration and travel restrictions / edited by MM Eboch.
Description: New York : Greenhaven Publishing, 2019. | Series: Introducing issues with
  opposing viewpoints | Includes bibliographical references and index. | Audience: Grades 7-12.
Identifiers: LCCN ISBN 9781534504233 (library bound) | ISBN 9781534504837 (pbk.)
Subjects: LCSH: Immigrants--United States--Juvenile literature. | United States--Emigration and
  immigration--Juvenile literature. | Immigrants--Government policy--United States—Juvenile
  literature. | United States--Emigration and immigration--Government policy--Juvenile literature.
Classification: LCC JV6465.I4654 2019 | DDC 304.8/73--dc23

Manufactured in the United States of America

Website: http://greenhavenpublishing.com

Contents

Foreword

Indulging in a wide spectrum of ideas, beliefs, and perspectives is a critical cornerstone of democracy. After all, it is often debates over differences of opinion, such as whether to legalize abortion, how to treat prisoners, or when to enact the death penalty, that shape our society and drive it forward. Such diversity of thought is frequently regarded as the hallmark of a healthy and civilized culture. As the Reverend Clifford Schutjer of the First Congregational Church in Mansfield, Ohio, declared in a 2001 sermon, "Surrounding oneself with only like-minded people, restricting what we listen to or read only to what we find agreeable is irresponsible. Refusing to entertain doubts once we make up our minds is a subtle but deadly form of arrogance." With this advice in mind, Introducing Issues with Opposing Viewpoints books aim to open readers' minds to the critically divergent views that comprise our world's most important debates.

Introducing Issues with Opposing Viewpoints simplifies for students the enormous and often overwhelming mass of material now available via print and electronic media. Collected in every volume is an array of opinions that capture the essence of a particular controversy or topic. Introducing Issues with Opposing Viewpoints books embody the spirit of nineteenth-century journalist Charles A. Dana's axiom: "Fight for your opinions, but do not believe that they contain the whole truth, or the only truth." Absorbing such contrasting opinions teaches students to analyze the strength of an argument and compare it to its opposition. From this process readers can inform and strengthen their own opinions, or be exposed to new information that will change their minds. Introducing Issues with Opposing Viewpoints is a mosaic of different voices. The authors are statesmen, pundits, academics, journalists, corporations, and ordinary people who have felt compelled to share their experiences and ideas in a public forum. Their words have been collected from newspapers, journals, books, speeches, interviews, and the internet, the fastest growing body of opinionated material in the world.

Introducing Issues with Opposing Viewpoints shares many of the well-known features of its critically acclaimed parent series, Opposing

Viewpoints. The articles allow readers to absorb and compare divergent perspectives. Active reading questions preface each viewpoint, requiring the student to approach the material thoughtfully and carefully. Photographs, charts, and graphs supplement each article. A thorough introduction provides readers with crucial background on an issue. An annotated bibliography points the reader toward articles, books, and websites that contain additional information on the topic. An appendix of organizations to contact contains a wide variety of charities, nonprofit organizations, political groups, and private enterprises that each hold a position on the issue at hand. Finally, a comprehensive index allows readers to locate content quickly and efficiently.

Introducing Issues with Opposing Viewpoints is also significantly different from Opposing Viewpoints. As the series title implies, its presentation will help introduce students to the concept of opposing viewpoints and learn to use this material to aid in critical writing and debate. The series' four-color, accessible format makes the books attractive and inviting to readers of all levels. In addition, each viewpoint has been carefully edited to maximize a reader's understanding of the content. Short but thorough viewpoints capture the essence of an argument. A substantial, thought-provoking essay question placed at the end of each viewpoint asks the student to further investigate the issues raised in the viewpoint, compare and contrast two authors' arguments, or consider how one might go about forming an opinion on the topic at hand. Each viewpoint contains sidebars that include at-a-glance information and handy statistics. A Facts About section located in the back of the book further supplies students with relevant facts and figures.

Following in the tradition of the Opposing Viewpoints series, Greenhaven Publishing continues to provide readers with invaluable exposure to the controversial issues that shape our world. As John Stuart Mill once wrote: "The only way in which a human being can make some approach to knowing the whole of a subject is by hearing what can be said about it by persons of every variety of opinion and studying all modes in which it can be looked at by every character of mind. No wise man ever acquired his wisdom in any mode but this." It is to this principle that Introducing Issues with Opposing Viewpoints books are dedicated.

Introduction

"In order to protect Americans, and to advance the national interest, the United States must ensure that those entering this country will not harm the American people subsequent to their entry...."

— US Department of Homeland
Security, January 27, 2017

Imagine you are heading away to college for at least four years. You expect to visit your family during the holidays, but then you get some bad news. If you leave the place where you're going to school, you'll never be able to return. You must choose between staying in school and seeing your family.

Imagine your town has been destroyed in a civil war or natural disaster. Your house is gone; friends and family members have been killed. It's hard to get medical help, food, or even safe drinking water. You want to move someplace where you can build a better life and not live in fear. You are willing to work hard, but you need a little help to get started. You apply to immigrate to a country that is often described as the land of opportunity. The country was built by immigrants, so surely they will welcome and respect immigrants. A famous monument there has greeted people with these words: "Give me your tired, your poor, Your huddled masses yearning to breathe free, The wretched refuse of your teeming shore." That sounds like a welcome. But then you discover that the country refuses to let anyone like you move there. You are not even allowed to visit, because of where you were born.

Imagine you're working at a busy international airport, where flights from foreign countries land. Your job is to screen the people coming off of those flights, trying to enter your country. You need to identify anyone who could be a criminal or a potential terrorist. The safety of your fellow citizens depends on your ability to stop terrorist attacks before they happen. But how can you tell who is dangerous? Not every country has an up-to-date database of people associated with crimes and suspicious activities. Even if they do, they may not share that information with your country. Some countries have unstable or corrupt governments. That makes it easier for people to get forged identity documents. You don't want to let someone in if you can't trust that the person is who they claim to be, and that you have accurate information about them. If you let a terrorist into your country, people could die.

Which is more important, a person's freedom to travel where and when they wish, a refugee's ability to find a safe home, or a country's responsibility to keep its citizens as safe as possible? How can all these things be reconciled in a way that works best for everyone?

These questions are complicated, but many people have strong opinions about them. Those opinions are not always backed by facts. Even when they are, the same facts may be interpreted in different ways. The same risks and rewards may be given different weight. Politicians try to make the rules, activists protest if they see treatment they believe to be unfair, and the courts decide what is allowed by law. In the end, rules may be approved or struck down based on the changes of just a few words. But lives are literally at stake.

Immigration and travel restrictions are not always related to terrorism and security. They also have been put into place throughout history because of public health concerns. A nation's government may issue recommendations for controlled movement of individuals with certain high-risk communicable diseases, such as Ebola, to contain the disease and avoid a potential pandemic. Reactions to attempts to restrict people from crossing borders for fears of a global pandemic are highly charged. There are those who say such travel and residency bans are ineffective. For instance, a twenty-three-year travel restriction on individuals with HIV/AIDS in the United States did nothing to stop the spread of that disease. Screening and diagnostic processes at airport checkpoints for diseases like HIV and Ebola are often rushed and erroneous and therefore ineffective. Research has found that flight bans imposed to prevent the spread of influenza may delay but not prevent the spread of such diseases. However, attempts to contain or stop the spread of threatening diseases can also be a savvy public relations move for a country's government intent on calming a nervous public. Proponents of health-related travel bans argue that it's better to be safe than sorry.

Immigration and travel restrictions have a long history in the United States, but they received greater attention recently. In January 2017, President Trump issued an executive order that would have banned immigrants and travelers from seven countries.

Many people, especially Democrats and others on the political left, criticized the ban. They claimed it was racist, because it targeted countries that were dominantly Muslim. As evidence, they point to a statement released by Trump's team in 2015 while he was running for president: "Donald J. Trump is calling for a total and complete shutdown of Muslims entering the United States until our country's representatives can figure out what the hell is going on." Later Trump changed his focus to territories connected to terrorism rather than all Muslims. Yet because he excluded some countries connected to terrorist activity and included others with no connections to terrorism, the accusations of racism continued.

President Trump, his allies, and some government officials stood by the ban. They claimed it was necessary for national security and would help prevent terrorism. The countries listed in the travel ban were accused of lacking the proper screening processes that could help US immigration determine who might be a criminal or a terrorist threat. Without detailed, accurate databases and secure forms of ID, such as fingerprinting, US immigration cannot identify and stop potential terrorists. The intent of the travel ban was to encourage those countries to provide better information, according to the people supporting it.

Opponents pointed out that the ban did not include any countries economically important to the United States, or to the Trump family business interests. For this reason, they argued that the ban was more about political posturing and economic effects than preventing terrorism.

In addition, critics suggested that the ban will not prevent terrorism, and may in fact make Americans less safe. They argued that a ban that seems to target Muslims will encourage more Islamist terrorists to retaliate against the United States. In addition, the original ban included Iraq, where the US military is active. Some people believed that banning immigrants from Iraq would harm the relationship between US and Iraqi forces working together.

The ban was challenged in federal courts in several states. The courts blocked implementation of the ban. President Trump issued a revised version of his executive order in March 2017. This version dropped Iraq after the country agreed to improve travel documentation and information sharing. The new ban also included other changes designed to address some of the critics' objections. The Supreme Court approved the ban, with certain limitations, but that did not stop the protests. The debate continues, along with court challenges.

This issue is explored from a variety of diverse perspectives in *Introducing Issues with Opposing Viewpoints: Immigration and Travel Restrictions*. The contributors in this resource examine the difficult question of how to balance travel and freedom with health and security in our increasingly dangerous world.

Chapter 1

Why Do Countries Restrict Immigration and Travel?

Traveling across national borders has become a complex practice in the years since 9/11.

A History of Immigration Legislation

Beth Rowen

"The Chinese Exclusion Act of 1882 bans 'skilled and unskilled laborers and Chinese employed in mining' from entering the country for ten years."

The following viewpoint offers a timeline of immigration history. The United States has passed laws controlling immigration for over two hundred years. Although the country was founded by immigrants and the descendents of immigrants, many laws were enacted in an effort to stop or reduce new immigration. In part, this was due to xenophobia, an intense dislike or fear of people from other countries. Sometimes racism was also a factor. Immigrants from northern Europe typically received preference over anyone else. Naturalization (allowing a foreigner to gain citizenship) was originally reserved for white people. Immigrants of African descent were allowed to become US citizens starting in 1870. Additional laws targeted other groups, such as Asians.

People could also be prevented from immigrating or becoming citizens for reasons other than race or nationality. Criminals, the mentally ill, and people with contagious diseases have been banned at various times. In the twentieth century, people were sometimes banned for political beliefs or homosexuality. Starting in 1980, refugees—people fleeing war, natural disaster, or persecution in their home country —were considered separately from immigrants. Laws also addressed expatriation, when a person chooses to live outside their native country or is banished from their country. Rowen is former managing editor of infoplease.com and factmonster.com.

AS YOU READ, CONSIDER THE FOLLOWING QUESTIONS:

1. When did the United States first pass laws about immigrants becoming citizens?
2. How could a person's physical or mental abilities affect their ability to immigrate?
3. How has fear played a part in immigration policy?

1790

The Naturalization Act of 1790, the country's first naturalization statute, says that unindentured white males must live in the US for two years before becoming citizens.

1795

The Naturalization Act of 1790 is amended and extends the residency requirement to five years.

1798

With xenophobia on the rise, the residency requirement in the Naturalization Act of 1790 is lengthened again, to 14 years.

1802

The residency requirement for citizenship is reduced to five years.

1819

The Steerage Act requires that ship captains must submit manifests with information about immigrants onboard to the Collector of Customs, the secretary of state, and Congress.

Female European immigrants being processed at Ellis Island at the turn of the twentieth century. Northern Europeans received preferential status.

1843

The American Republican party is formed in New York (it later becomes known as the Native American party) by citizens opposed to the increased number of immigrants in the US. The nativists, or members of the Know-Nothing Movement, seek to permit only native-born Americans to run for office and try to raise the residency requirement to 25 years.

1868

Congress passed the Expatriation Act of 1868 that said "the right of expatriation is a natural and inherent right of all people." The act was intended to protect the rights of naturalized immigrants whose native countries did not recognize expatriation claims.

1870
The Naturalization Act of 1870 allows "aliens of African nativity" and "persons of African descent" to become US citizens.

1875
The Page Act becomes law. It's the country's first exclusionary act, banning criminals, prostitutes, and Chinese contract laborers from entering the country.

1882
Congress passes the Immigration Act. The law imposes a $.50 tax on new arrivals and bans "convicts (except those convicted of political offenses), lunatics, idiots and persons likely to become public charges" from entering the US.

The Chinese Exclusion Act of 1882 bans "skilled and unskilled laborers and Chinese employed in mining" from entering the country for ten years and denies Chinese immigrants the path to citizenship. Thousands of Chinese immigrants had worked on the construction of the Trans-Continental Railroad, and these workers were left unemployed when the project was complete. The high rate of unemployment and anti-Chinese sentiment led to passage of the law.

1888
Congress passes the Scott Act, which amends the Chinese Exclusion Act. It bans Chinese workers from re-entering the US after they left.

1891
Immigration Act of 1891 creates the Bureau of Immigration, which falls under the Treasury Department. The act also calls for the deportation of people who entered the country illegally and denies entry for polygamists, the mentally ill, and those with contagious diseases.

1892
The Geary Act strengthens the Chinese Exclusion Act of 1882 by requiring Chinese laborers to carry a resident permit at all times.

Failure to do so could result in deportation or a sentence to hard labor. It also extends for another 10 years the ban on Chinese becoming citizens.

Ellis Island opens. It served as the primary immigration station of the US between 1892 and 1954, processing some 12 million immigrants. By some estimates, 40% of all Americans have a relative who passed through Ellis Island.

1903
Congress passes the Anarchist Exclusion Act, which denies anarchists, other political extremists, beggars, and epileptics entry into the US. It's the first time individuals are banned from the US based on political beliefs.

1906
The Naturalization Act of 1906 creates the Bureau of Immigration and Naturalization and places it under the jurisdiction of the Commerce Department. The act also requires immigrants to learn English before they can become citizens.

1907
The Immigration Act of 1907 broadens the categories of people banned from immigrating to the US. The list excludes "imbeciles," "feeble-minded" people, those with physical or mental disabilities that prevent them from working, tuberculosis victims, children who enter the US without parents, and those who committed crimes of "moral turpitude."

The "Gentleman's Agreement" between the US and Japan ends the immigration of Japanese workers.

Congress passes the Expatriation Act of 1907 that says women must adopt the citizenship of their husbands. Therefore, women who marry foreigners lose their US citizenship unless their husbands become citizens.

1917
Immigration Act of 1917, also called Asiatic Barred Zone Act, further restricted immigration, particularly of people from a large swath of

Asia and the Pacific Islands. The act also bars homosexuals, "idiots," "feeble-minded persons," "criminals," "insane persons," alcoholics, and other categories. In addition, the act sets a literacy standard for immigrants age 16 and older. They must be able to read a 40-word selection in their native language.

1921
The Emergency Quota Law of 1921 limits the number of immigrants entering the US each year to 350,000 and implements a nationality quota. Immigration from any country is capped at 3% of the population of that nationality based on the 1910 census. The law reduces immigration from eastern and southern Europe while favoring immigrants from Northern Europe.

1922
Congress passes the Married Women's Act of 1922, also known as the "Cable Act." It repeals the provision of the Expatriation Act of 1907 that revoked the citizenship of women who married foreigners.

1924
The National Origins Act reduces the number of immigrants entering the US each year to 165,000 and the nationality quota set forth in the Quota Law of 1921 is cut to 2% of the population of that nationality based on the 1890 census. The quota system did not apply to immigrants from the western hemisphere.

The US Border Patrol is created.

1929
The National Origins Act once again reduces the annaul cap on the number of immigrants allowed to enter the US, this time to 150,000. The 2% quota is linked to 1920 census data, thereby further limiting the number of immigrants from eastern and southern Europe.

1940
The Alien Registration Act (Smith Act) requires that all immigrants age 14 and up register with the government and be fingerprinted. The act also bans individuals considered "subversives" from immigrating.

1942

Because so many American men are fighting in World War II, the US faced a shortage of farm workers and begins hiring Mexican workers in what was known as the bracero program. About 5 million Mexican workers participate in the program.

1943

The Chinese Exclusion Repeal Act allows Chinese workers to immigrate to the US, but with an annual quota of 105.

1946

The Chinese Exclusion Repeal Act is broadened to cover Filipinos and Indians, essentially repealing the Immigration Act of 1917.

1948

The Displaced Persons Act allows up to 200,000 refugees displaced by World War II to enter the US.

1950

Internal Security Act allows the deportation of any immigrants who were ever members of the Communist Party.

1952

Immigration and Nationality Act of 1952 (the McCarran-Walter Act) consolidates earlier immigration legislation into one law and eliminates race as a basis of exclusion. However, race continues to be a factor because the quota system remains in place, except for immigrants from the western hemisphere. Immigration from any country is capped at 1/6th of 1% of the population of that nationality based on the 1920 census.

1965

The Immigration Act of 1965 gets rid of the nationality quotas, but limits annual immigration from the eastern hemisphere to 170,000, with a limit of 20,000 immigrants per country, and for the first time caps annual immigration from the western hemisphere at 120,000, without the country limit. In addition, a preference system is established for family members of US citizens.

1966
Cuban Adjustment Act allows Cubans to apply for permanent resident status after residing in the US for two years.

1975
At the end of the Vietnam War, the US passes the Indochina Migration and Refugee Assistance Act of 1975 that resettles about 200,000 Vietnamese and Cambodian refugees in the US and gives them a special parole status. The program was extended to Laotians in 1976.

1978
The immigration caps outlined in the 1965 Immigration Act are replaced with an overall annual limit of 290,000.

1980
The Refugee Act defines refugees as a person who flees his or her country "on account of race, religion, nationality, or political opinion." Refugees are considered a different category than immigrants. The president and Congress are granted the authority to establish an annual ceiling on the number of refugees allowed into the US. The act also lowers the annual limit of immigrants to 270,000, from 290,000.

1986
The Immigration Reform and Control Act of 1986 (IRCA) allows immigrants who had entered the US before Jan. 1, 1982, to apply for legal status but required them to pay fines, fees, and back taxes. It also gives the same rights to immigrants who worked in agricultural jobs for 90 days before May 1982. About 3 million immigrants gained legal status through the law. The act also requires employers to verify work status of all new hires and fine those who hire undocumented workers.

1990

The Immigration Act of 1990 sets an annual ceiling of 700,000 immigrants for three years, and 675,000 thereafter.

1996

The Illegal Immigration Reform and Immigrant Responsibility Act broadens the definition of "aggravated felony" and increases the number of crimes classified as such so immigrants could be deported for a wider range of crimes. The law is applied retroactively. The act also increased the number of Border Patrol agents and established an "expedited removal" procedure to deport immigrants without a formal hearing.

Personal Responsibility and Work Opportunity Reconciliation Act sharply cuts legal permanent residents' eligibility for many public-assistance benefits, including food stamps, Supplemental Security Income (SSI), Temporary Assistance for Needy Families (TANF), and Medicaid.

2005

The REAL ID Act of 2005 requires states to verify a person's immigration status or citizenship before issuing licenses, expands restrictions on refugees requesting asylum, and limits the habeas corpus rights of immigrants.

2006

The REAL ID Act of 2005 requires states to verify a person's immigration status or citizenship before issuing licenses, expands restrictions on refugees requesting asylum, and limits the habeas corpus rights of immigrants.

2014

On Nov. 20, 2014, President Barack Obama announced he was taking executive action to delay the deportation of some 5 million illegal immigrants. Under the new policy people who are parents of US citizens or legal residents will receive deportation deferrals and authorization to work legally if they have been in the US for more than five years and pass background checks.

Obama's action also amended the 2012 Deferred Action for Childhood Arrivals program, which allows people under age 31 who were brought to the US as children to apply for two-year deportation deferrals and work permits. Obama's policy change lifted the age ceiling and added a year to the deferral period. Twenty-six states challenged the executive order, and in February 2015 a federal judge issued a preliminary injunction, temporarily blocking the provisions of the executive order while the states pursued a lawsuit to permanently shut down the program.

2017
In an ongoing legal battle, the White House attempted to impose iterative restrictions on immigration from several Muslim-majority countries in conflicted regions. Successful legal challenges from different states and cities saw a significant decrease in the scope of the immigration orders, though the administration would eventually implement an executive order that withstood constitutional scrutiny. Opponents of the measure claimed that it was motivated by Islamophobia, while proponents argued it was valuable to national security.

2018
Since his election, President Donald J. Trump made several efforts to fulfill his campaign promise of an extensive border wall. This costly security measure drew a wide range of criticisms, and sparked contentious debates surrounding the nature of US border protections. During this time the White House declared its intentions of phasing out the DACA program passed by President Obama. Republicans and Democrats both were called on to pass a replacement program by a proposed deadline of March 5. However, party members were unable to reach a consensus, and many beneficiaries of DACA were put into legal/political limbo.

The US Border Patrol was created in 1924 and expanded in 1996. Its priority mission is preventing terrorists and terrorist weapons from entering the United States.

EVALUATING THE AUTHOR'S ARGUMENTS:

This viewpoint presents a timeline of immigration law, rather than a personal opinion or argument. What do these laws tell you about the attitudes Americans had toward immigrants in the past? What has changed and what remains the same?

Viewpoint

2

Travel Bans as a Means to Protecting Public Health

Suzanne B. Goldberg

"The trend has been increasingly for countries to abandon their policies of exclusion."

In the following viewpoint, written in the late 1990s, Suzanne B. Goldberg notes some of the reasons travel and immigration to the United States have been restricted. She then focuses on HIV status. In 1987, when HIV and AIDS were poorly understood, America restricted the entry of people who were HIV-positive. Specifics of the law changed over the years, and the ban was ended in 2010, after this viewpoint was written. While some countries continue to ban or restrict people with HIV, many other countries have dropped such laws. Countries that ban people with HIV cite public health risks and the expense of caring for infected people. Other countries follow the recommendations of public health organizations. They believe a ban is unnecessary, is discriminatory, and is counterproductive to public health. Goldberg is executive vice president for university life at Columbia University, and director of the Center for Gender & Sexuality Law at Columbia Law School.

"Immigration Issues and Travel Restrictions," by Suzanne B. Goldberg, Remedy Health Media, LLC, 1998. Reprinted by permission.

AS YOU READ, CONSIDER THE FOLLOWING QUESTIONS:
1. How does immigration differ from travel?
2. What are some risks of allowing people with contagious diseases to immigrate?
3. What is the difference between a "dangerous contagious disease" and a "communicable disease of public health significance"?

Immigration refers to the permanent resettlement of an individual from one country to another, either with legal authorization or without. Travel refers to shorter stays that are intended to be temporary. Both immigration and travel are subject to a variety of restrictions in countries throughout the world, and immigration has often been a source of social and political controversy. The government's ability to restrict entry is rooted in the core principle of national sovereignty that every nation has a basic right to protect itself by controlling its borders.

Among the long-standing grounds of inadmissibility have been health-related reasons, along with disfavored political views, affiliations with terrorist organizations, involvement in international political conflicts, convictions for certain types of crimes, and personal characteristics such as sexual orientation. In the United States, a federal law, known as the Immigration and Nationality Act (INA), sets the terms for who may be admitted and lists several of these grounds.

Since 1987, the United States has banned noncitizens with HIV from entering the country without a special waiver. Regardless of HIV status, every person who is not a US citizen must establish that he or she is admissible to receive official permission, by a visa or otherwise, to enter the United States for any length of time. Few issues in US immigration law have caused as much controversy as this exclusion. The reasons behind it are complex, reflecting ignorance and bias about HIV together with insular instincts that long have shaped the entire body of US immigration law.

The key ground of inadmissibility for people with HIV is found in one provision of the INA, as amended, that requires exclusion of any noncitizen who is determined to have a "communicable disease of public health significance." The law specifies that HIV is such a

People Living with HIV

As of the end of 2017, about 36.7 million people were living with HIV (Human Immunodeficiency Virus) around the world, of which 2.1 million were newly infected in 2015.

POPULATION OF PEOPLE LIVING WITH HIV IN 2015

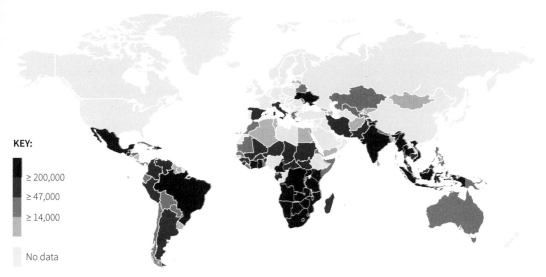

KEY:

≥ 200,000

≥ 47,000

≥ 14,000

No data

This graphic illustrates the parts of the world with the highest numbers of people with HIV. Critics of HIV travel bans contend that such restrictions are discriminatory and do not affect the spread of the disease.

disease, rendering any noncitizen with HIV inadmissible, absent an official waiver of the ground of inadmissibility. Since 1987, when HIV was added to the exclusion list, the US government has mandated HIV testing of all applicants for immigrant visas, refugee status, legalization, and adjustment of status. Although those seeking nonimmigrant visas, such as visitors' visas, were not subject to mandatory testing, the government has been permitted to test if it suspects that a nonimmigrant is infected.

In 1989, the Immigration Naturalization Service (INS) detained Hans Paul Verhoef, a Dutch citizen who sought to enter the United States to attend an international AIDS conference. Subsequently, a wide range of international organizations, including the World Health Organization, as well as members of Congress and public interest groups condemned the HIV ban as irrational and without public health justification. Additionally, several international organizations announced a boycott of the Sixth International AIDS Conference, held in the United States in June 1990, to protest the US policy. Defenders of the ban, however, urged that the public health would be endangered from the increased risk of HIV transmission by noncitizens and that the US health care system could be bankrupted by the demands of noncitizens with AIDS. In response, the administration of President George Bush created a temporary, ten-day waiver for persons attending academic, professional, or scientific conferences, which did not require that applicants state first whether they are HIV-positive.

In October 1990, the Immigration Act of 1990 (IMMACT 90), which amended the INA, was passed, altering the earlier language of the exclusion provision from "dangerous contagious disease" to "communicable disease of public health significance." The US Department of Health and Human Services then attempted to remove HIV and several other conditions from the exclusion list because such diseases are not transmitted by casual contact, through the air, or through common vehicles such as food or water and because they do not place the general population at risk. A public backlash prevented the removal of HIV from the exclusion list, and in May 1993, Congress approved legislation codifying the exclusion of HIV-infected aliens, which President Bill Clinton signed into law despite campaign promises to the contrary. IMMACT 90 did, however, provide the US attorney general discretion to grant exclusion waivers so long as the waiver applicant satisfies certain criteria pertaining to, for example, stage of illness, length of visit, and insurance coverage. These waivers have been typically issued for athletic events, medical conferences, and short-term visits.

Applicants for immigrant visas (those who seek to remain in the United States) have been held to a much higher standard. Prospective immigrants are eligible to apply for a waiver only if they are the spouse, unmarried son or daughter, or parent of a US citizen or lawful permanent resident. The immigrant waiver application process involves a complete medical exam, an application, and an interview. Under 1996 changes to the immigration law, applicants must meet stringent requirements to prove they have the financial resources to avoid

becoming public charges dependent upon the government for health care expenses.

Although the United States has maintained its HIV ban, many other nations have eliminated such restrictions on those entering their borders, following the recommendations of international and domestic public health organizations that a ban is unnecessary and even counterproductive to public health. Indeed, several nations have denounced discrimination against HIV-positive individuals in the immigration context. France and the United Kingdom have admitted noncitizens with HIV as have, for example, Costa Rica, South Africa, and Thailand, all of which lifted HIV exclusion laws and policies.

Russia, Qatar, and the United Arab Emirates are among the few countries that absolutely ban people with HIV from entering their borders. According to a list compiled by the US State Department, a substantial number of countries—for example, Belarus, China, Guyana, Hungary, and Saudi Arabia—do not apply an across-the-board ban but instead restrict the entry of people with HIV who seek to remain in the country for more than three to six months or who seek to become students or permanent residents. Other countries require visitors to take an HIV test, but only for lengthy visits, to obtain a work permit, or to apply for citizenship. To defend their restrictions, these countries make arguments similar to those advanced by the proponents of the US HIV ban. In particular, they argue that the introduction of foreigners with HIV is likely to increase transmission within the country. Some hold the view that gay Europeans and Americans, in particular, pose a danger, based on their belief that most Western gay men have HIV and are extremely promiscuous. In addition, the bans' defenders maintain that few or none of those with HIV take adequate precautions to avoid the risk of transmission. To some extent, fear of excessive public health expenditures for foreigners with HIV also motivates the restrictions. Still, the trend has been increasingly for countries to abandon their policies of exclusion.

On a different note, the INS recognized in 1996 that persecution based on HIV may be a basis for granting an individual asylum in the United States. Asylum law provides that a person who is unable to return to his or her home country because of past persecution or a well-founded fear of future persecution on account of race, religion, nationality, membership in a particular social group, or political opinion is eligible to seek asylum (and thus remain lawfully) in the United States. People with HIV may qualify for asylum if they can demonstrate that their home government (or a nongovernmental group that their government is unable or unwilling to control) causes "extreme harm" to those who are HIV infected. The INS has noted specifically, however, that inadequate medical treatment and social ostracism by themselves do not amount to persecution. Those who qualify for asylum are eligible to seek a waiver of the HIV exclusion on humanitarian grounds.

EVALUATING THE AUTHOR'S ARGUMENTS:

In this viewpoint, Suzanne B. Goldberg examines countries that ban people with HIV from entering or immigrating. Does the author seem to favor or disapprove of these bans? Does the information provided convince you one way or the other?

Viewpoint

3

A Travel Ban Won't Solve the Ebola Crisis

Tara Culp-Ressler

"The policies that give people a sense of security aren't always the ones that get the best results from a global health perspective."

In the following viewpoint, Tara Culp-Ressler discusses immigration and health risks as related to Ebola. Although the first cases of the virus happened in 1976, Ebola got its name during a huge outbreak that started in 2014. Over 28,000 people were infected between 2014 and 2016, and more than 11,000 of them died. The vast majority of the victims were in African countries, but a few cases reached other countries, including the United States This led to panic over the possibility of the epidemic sweeping America. However, the author argues that a travel ban would do more harm than good. She argues that it would not stop the spread of Ebola, but it would harm the world's ability to control the disease where it is now. In addition, trying to cut off some countries from the rest of the world would cause economic harm to them. Culp-Ressler is a senior editor at ThinkProgress.

"4 Reasons Why A Travel Ban Won't Solve The Ebola Crisis," by Tara Culp-Ressler, This material was created by the Centre for American Progress (americanprogress.org), October 16, 2014. Reprinted by permission.

Now that two health workers have contracted Ebola on US soil, and evidence has emerged that hospital officials weren't properly trained to contain the spread of the deadly virus, public panic about the global epidemic is intensifying. The director of the Centers for Disease Control and Prevention (CDC), Thomas Frieden, will testify at a congressional hearing on Thursday, during which he'll likely face tough questions about why the US hasn't halted flights from the Western African region that's been hardest hit by Ebola.

An increasing number of lawmakers on both sides of the aisle, as well as some former Obama administration officials, are calling for implementing a travel ban—a policy that also has the support of two thirds of the American public, according to the latest polling. On Wednesday, House Speaker John Boehner became the highest-ranking Republican to suggest that President Obama should impose temporary travel restrictions on flights from the affected region.

Banning flights from Ebola-stricken countries sounds like a logical step to contain the spread of an outbreak that's been spiraling out of control in West Africa for months. But the policies that give people a sense of security aren't always the ones that get the best results from a global health perspective. Experts say there are a couple significant reasons why travel bans are actually the wrong approach:

1. It will prevent health officials from being able to effectively track people with symptoms.

The CDC's Frieden has been firmly opposed to a travel ban from the start, and has repeatedly explained that such restrictions will

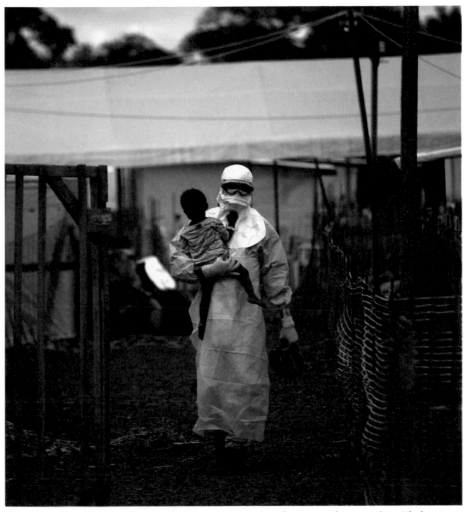

However well intentioned, imposing a travel ban to combat an epidemic such as Ebola may do more harm than good because it limits accessibility of health care workers who want to offer their assistance.

undermine one of the best tools we have to contain the epidemic: The ability to track people's movements. "Even when governments restrict travel and trade, people in affected countries still find a way to move and it is even harder to track them systematically," he wrote in an op-ed earlier this month.

Right now, government officials can coordinate with airport security to figure out where Ebola-infected people may have traveled before and after they started displaying symptoms. That's something the US infrastructure is well-equipped to do. If travel becomes less systematic, however, airports won't serve as the same kind of resource. Considering the fact that the World Health Organization (WHO) has said that the failure to effectively track patients has been one of the biggest reasons that Liberia hasn't been able to contain Ebola, this is not a direction we want to go in.

2. It will only delay the inevitable spread of Ebola while the outbreak continues in West African countries.

Travel bans are a temporary solution. We can't suspend air travel from West Africa forever, and even if we do, it would certainly be possible to fly to another country first before landing in the US. (The Liberian man who was diagnosed with Ebola in Dallas, for instance, flew from Belgium.) The policy would simply be delaying the inevitable in order to make Americans feel safer for a few weeks.

According to Alex Vespignani, a physicist at Northeastern University who developed a computer model to predict how air traffic can influence the spread of Ebola, an 80 percent reduction in air traffic only delays the risk of an Ebola-infected passenger coming to the US for about four weeks. A 90 percent reduction would delay it for another month or so. "We're a little safer for a finite amount of time, but then you are not really solving the problem," Vespignani explained to Forbes.

3. It will become a logistical nightmare.

Health experts have maintained that sealing off the countries affected by the Ebola outbreak would actually make it more difficult to address the virus at its source. Travel restrictions could hamper efforts to get critical medical supplies into Western African countries, as well as restrict the movements of medical personnel who are needed on the ground in Liberia, Guinea, and Sierra Leone.

Even if the US implemented a more nuanced policy that exempted doctors and aid workers from the travel ban, it would still be too difficult to coordinate in practice. Who would decide who gets approved to travel? How long would the application process take? As Vox recently reported, responding to humanitarian crises is complicated and messy, and we can't afford to slow down the process by putting obstacles in front of a Doctors Without Borders volunteer who's trying to get to and from Liberia.

In fact, workers with Doctors Without Borders say that the current scarcity of flights is already impeding their work as they coordinate with 240 international staff members currently in West Africa. "We need the flights to operate. That's the bottom line," Tim Shenk, the press officer for the group, told the Detroit Free Press.

4. It could destabilize the countries at the heart of the outbreak.

Limiting travel can lead to lasting economic consequences for the countries that are cut off from the rest of the world. For instance, in 2006, the World Bank estimated that a potential international flu pandemic could lead to a $1.5 trillion reduction in global gross domestic product—and two thirds of that number represents the cost of people restricting their movements and avoiding traveling to infected countries. The World Health Organization may put that figure even higher. According to WHO's estimates, recently cited by director general Dr. Margaret Chan, about 90 percent of the economic costs of outbreaks "come from irrational and disorganized efforts of the public to avoid infection."

Plus, the researchers who have examined the effects of the 2003 SARS outbreak say quarantining people within an infected country is often an overly broad approach that can end up facilitating social and political unrest. In Liberia and Sierra Leone, which are not incredibly stable countries to begin with, that could actually allow the virus to spread even further in the impoverished region.

"If we completely isolate them… we know from experience with public health, that marginalizes them," Anthony S. Fauci, the director of the National Institute of Allergy and Infectious Disease, recently explained on Fox News. "You can have civil unrest, governments can fall. Then you wind up having spread of the virus to other countries in West Africa, which would only compound the problem."

If the things that the CDC has been doing aren't working, and if health workers aren't educated about the proper protocols to prevent Ebola transmissions, that obviously needs to change. The federal agency has already taken some steps to ensure that what happened in Dallas won't happen again; it has issued stricter guidelines for American hospitals dealing with Ebola patients, and is preparing to deploy emergency teams to any areas that report new infections. The second health worker has also been transferred to one of the four hospitals in the country equipped with a special isolation unit, something that might become standard protocol if more Americans become infected with Ebola in the future.

But there's a fine line between holding federal health officials accountable and pursuing policies simply to give Americans the illusion of safety. After all, as political figures remain singularly focused on what we should be doing to prevent Ebola here at home, the risks here are still incredibly low, and the real crisis continues to worsen in Liberia—which just declared a shortage of body bags, dire news that's mostly been buried under the headlines about Dallas.

EVALUATING THE AUTHOR'S ARGUMENTS:

In this viewpoint, Tara Culp-Ressler argues that banning flights from countries with Ebola is a bad idea. She quotes experts including scientists and representatives of the Centers for Disease Control and Prevention and the World Health Organization. How does this use of expert viewpoints support her claims?

The Facts on President Trump's Travel Ban

US Department of Homeland Security

"The United States must ensure that those entering this country will not harm the American people subsequent to their entry."

The following viewpoint is a fact sheet from the US Department of Homeland Security. It describes the March 6, 2017, executive order issued by President Trump. This executive order followed an earlier one, which was commonly called a travel ban or Muslim ban. That executive order was widely criticized in the media and challenged in court. It was replaced by a slightly altered version. This fact sheet describes the goal of the executive order as protecting Americans from terrorism. It planned for a ninety-day suspension of travel from certain countries in the Middle East and Northern Africa. During that time, the Department of Homeland Security planned to review those countries' visa policies and request changes.

"Fact Sheet: Protecting The Nation From Foreign Terrorist Entry To The United States," US Department of Homeland Security, January 29, 2017. Reprinted by permission.

1. What does the fact sheet say is the primary goal of this executive order?
2. What does section 212(f) of the Immigration and Nationality Act (INA) allow the president to do?
3. How did the executive order plan to treat lawful permanent residents of the United States differently from other travelers from the countries in question?

On March 6, 2017, President Trump issued a new Executive Order on Executive Order Protecting The Nation From Foreign Terrorist Entry Into The United States that rescinded the Executive Order that was issued on January 27, 2017.

The Executive Order signed on January 27, 2017, allows for the proper review and establishment of standards to prevent terrorist or criminal infiltration by foreign nationals. The United States has the world's most generous immigration system, yet it has been repeatedly exploited by terrorists and other malicious actors who seek to do us harm. In order to ensure that the United States government can conduct a thorough and comprehensive analysis of the national security risks posed from our immigration system, it imposes a 90-day suspension on entry to the United States of nationals of certain designated countries—countries that were designated by Congress and the Obama Administration as posing national security risks in the Visa Waiver Program.

In order to protect Americans, and to advance the national interest, the United States must ensure that those entering this country will not harm the American people subsequent to their entry, and that they do not bear n\malicious intent toward the United States and its people. The Executive Order protects the United States from countries compromised by terrorism and ensures a more rigorous vetting process. This Executive Order ensures that we have a functional immigration system that safeguards our national security.

This Executive Order, as well as the two issued earlier in the week, provide the Department with additional resources, tools and personnel

Over the years, technology such as digital fingerprint scanners has been employed at US airport customs points to increase security measures.

to carry out the critical work of securing our borders, enforcing the immigration laws of our nation, and ensuring that individuals who pose a threat to national security or public safety cannot enter or remain in our country. Protecting the American people is the highest priority of our government and this Department.

The Department of Homeland Security will faithfully execute the immigration laws and the President's Executive Order, and we will treat all of those we encounter humanely and with professionalism.

Authorities

The Congress provided the President of the United States, in section 212(f) of the Immigration and Nationality Act (INA), with the authority to suspend the entry of any class of aliens the president deems detrimental to the national interest. This authority has been exercised by nearly every president since President Carter, and has been a component of immigration laws since the enactment of the INA in 1952.

Action

For the next 90 days, nearly all travelers, except US citizens, traveling on passports from Iraq, Syria, Sudan, Iran, Somalia, Libya, and Yemen will be temporarily suspended from entry to the United States. The 90 day period will allow for proper review and establishment of standards to prevent terrorist or criminal infiltration by foreign nationals.

Importantly, however, Lawful Permanent Residents of the United States traveling on a valid I-551 will be allowed to board US bound aircraft and will be assessed for exceptions at arrival ports of entry, as appropriate. The entry of these individuals, subject to national security checks, is in the national interest. Therefore, we expect swift entry for these individuals.

In the first 30 days, DHS will perform a global country-by-country review of the information each country provides when their citizens apply for a US visa or immigration benefit. Countries will then have 60 days to comply with any requests from the US government to update or improve the quality of the information they provide.

DHS and the Department of State have the authority, on a case-by-case basis, to issue visas or allow the entry of nationals of these countries into the United States when it serves the national interest. These seven countries were designated by Congress and the Obama Administration as posing a significant enough security risk to warrant additional scrutiny in the visa waiver context.

The Refugee Admissions Program will be temporarily suspended for the next 120 days while DHS and interagency partners review screening procedures to ensure refugees admitted in the future do not pose a security risk to citizens of the United States.

The Executive Order does not prohibit entry of, or visa issuance to, travelers with diplomatic visas, North Atlantic Treaty Organization visas, C-2 visas for travel to the United Nations, and G-1, G-2, G-3, and G-4 visas.

The Department of Homeland Security along with the Department of State, the Office of the Director of National Intelligence, and the Federal Bureau of Investigation will develop uniform screening standards for all immigration programs government-wide.

Upon resumption of the US Refugee Admissions Program, refugee admissions to the United States will not exceed 50,000 for fiscal year 2017.

The Secretary of Homeland Security will expedite the completion and implementation of a biometric entry-exit tracking system of all travelers into the United States.

Federal Government

As part of a broader set of government actions, the Secretary of State will review all nonimmigrant visa reciprocity agreements to ensure that they are, with respect to each visa classification, truly reciprocal.

The Department of State will restrict the Visa Interview Waiver Program and require additional nonimmigrant visa applicants to undergo an in-person interview.

Transparency

The Department of Homeland Security, in order to be more transparent with the American people, and to more effectively implement policies and practices that serve the national interest will make information available to the public every 180 days. In coordination with the Department of Justice, DHS will provide information regarding the number of foreign nationals charged with terrorism-related offense or gender-based violence against women while in the United States.

The Revised Travel Ban Made Subtle Exceptions

Tom McCarthy

"The new ban does not apply to permanent US residents or to citizens of Iraq— although 'additional scutiny' is called for in the latter case."

In the following viewpoint, Tom McCarthy explains some details of the revised version of President Trump's executive order. The original order barred people from seven countries from entering the US for ninety days. These countries, Iran, Iraq, Syria, Yemen, Somalia, Sudan and Libya, all had populations that were primarily Muslim. For this reason, the ban was sometimes referred to as a "Muslim ban." That version also banned Syrian refugees indefinitely. The executive order was blocked by federal courts. The revised ban removed Iraq from the list of countries and lifted the indefinite ban on Syrian refugees. These changes were in response to the legal challenges to the original executive order. The author goes on to list people who should not be affected by the ban. McCarthy is national affairs correspondent for Guardian US.

AS YOU READ, CONSIDER THE FOLLOWING QUESTIONS:
1. Are "green card holders"—lawful permanent US residents—affected by the ban?
2. How are close family members of US citizens affected by the ban?
3. Are international organizations affected by the ban?

For his second pass at an executive order temporarily banning travel to the United States from Muslim-majority countries, Donald Trump has made some basic revisions. Unlike the original travel ban, issued in January, the new ban does not apply to permanent US residents or to citizens of Iraq—although "additional scrutiny" is called for in the latter case.

The new ban, which you can read here, makes subtler exceptions, too. Here is a list of groups not covered by the ban issued Monday, according to the fine print.

Note: if you are planning travel to the United States and are concerned about your status, consult with a legal professional.

- **Lawful permanent US residents**—i.e., green-card holders.
- **People inside the United States.** The ban only applies to people who are abroad at the time of the order.
- **Valid visa holders.** The ban does not apply to people who currently have a valid visa for travel to the United States or who had a valid visa before the date of the original ban (27 January 2017).
- **People with other valid documents.** These include holders of diplomatic visas and of documents that are not visas but that permit travel to the United States, such as "advance parole" documents, which can allow entry to the US for humanitarian reasons.
- **Certain non-US citizens who are dual nationals.** A dual national from a "country of particular concern" (to be defined in a worldwide review within 20 days) may be exempted from the ban if the person is traveling on a passport issued by a non-designated country.

Thousands of activists flocked to JFK airport in New York City to protest President Trump's Muslim travel ban in January 2017.

- **Asylum-holders, previously admitted refugees** and individuals who have been granted protection under the Convention Against Torture.
- **Hardship cases.** Officials may grant waivers on a case-by-case basis "if the foreign national has demonstrated to the officer's satisfaction that denying entry during the suspension period would cause undue hardship, and that his or her entry would not pose a threat to national security and would be in the national interest."

Nine kinds of hardship cases are contemplated:

1. **People caught temporarily outside the United States.** This clause establishes a waiver for foreign nationals who have "previously been admitted to the United States for a continuous period of work, study, or other long-term activity" but who were outside the United States when the order came into effect.

2. **People with "previously established significant contacts with the United States"** who were outside the United States when the order came into effect.

3. **People with significant business or professional obligations inside the United States.**

4. **Close family members of US citizens, lawful residents or visa holders.** The waiver is for foreign nationals who wish to visit or live with their US loved one.

5. **The most vulnerable.** This group includes anyone who is an "infant, a young child or adoptee, an individual needing urgent medical care, or someone whose entry is otherwise justified by the special circumstances of the case."

6. **Current or former US government employees.** This group would include some foreign nationals who have worked with the US military in war zones.

7. **International Organizations Immunities Act travelers.** That includes members of about 75 groups including the United Nations, the International Atomic Energy Agency, the International Monetary Fund, the International Committee of the Red Cross.

8. **Landed Canadians:** "the foreign national is a landed Canadian immigrant who applies for a visa at a location within Canada."

9. **Government-sponsored exchange visitors.**

EVALUATING THE AUTHOR'S ARGUMENTS:

Viewpoint author Tom McCarthy describes people who will *not* be affected by the executive order banning travel from certain countries. What is the likely purpose of focusing on those who should be exempt from the travel ban?

Chapter 2

Is President Trump's Travel Ban Racist or Necessary?

President Trump issued an executive order that restricted the entry of people traveling from certain nations.

Viewpoint

1

Reaction to the Travel Ban

Clark Mindock

"We will be arguing Friday in the Fourth Circuit that the ban should ultimately be struck down."

In the following viewpoint, Clark Mindock traces the history of President Trump's so-called "travel ban" and analyzes the responses to it. At the time this viewpoint was written, the Supreme Court had approved the latest version of the ban. However, lower courts were still considering arguments that the ban was illegal. While White House officials were pleased with the Supreme Court response, some groups were not. The ACLU, a nonprofit organization that works to protect individual rights, issued a statement against the ban. The group accused president Trump of prejudice and argued that the travel ban was unfair. Mindock is a US reporter at the *Independent*, a British news source.

AS YOU READ, CONSIDER THE FOLLOWING QUESTIONS:
1. How can this travel ban be considered persecution against Muslims?
2. Why did legal experts expect the Supreme Court to rule in favor of the administration and against those challenging the ban?
3. How did civil rights groups react to the passage of the travel ban?

"Travel Ban: What is Trump's major immigration policy, and why is it called a 'Muslim ban'? All you need to know," by Clark Mindock, Independent Digital News & Media, December 5, 2017. Reprinted by permission.

Many Americans believed Trump's travel ban was discriminatory and took to the streets to protest it.

President Donald Trump's controversial travel ban is set to go forward after the Supreme Court ruled this week in favour of the beleaguered measure.

The ban's legal future remains a little unclear, however, as two US appeals courts are set to hear arguments against the ban, which is the third of its kind proposed by Mr Trump.

Just two Supreme Court justices voted against allowing the travel ban to go through. Liberal Justices Ruth Bader Ginsberg and Sonia Sotomayor were the two hold-outs on the nine-judge panel.

What Is in the Ban?

Mr Trump's latest ban targets travellers from Chad, Iran, Libya, Somalia, Syria, and Yemen. It restricts admission into the US from those countries unless the individual travelling can prove they have a "bona fide" relationship with someone in the United States.

The bans have all included restrictive language on refugee admission as well, and have resulted in significant cuts to those programmes this year.

What Is the Argument against the Ban?

Last year, while Mr Trump was campaigning to become president, he repeatedly called for what he then described as a ban on Muslim people from coming into the US. Since the countries targeted by the travel ban are predominantly Muslim, lower courts have frequently ruled that the ban was intended to persecute members of a particular religion instead of for national security.

The Trump administration has argued in the courts that the President has a de facto concern with national security—and the Supreme Court has ruled in favour of a previous ban with that responsibility in mind.

What's Next for the Travel Ban?

While the Supreme Court ruled in favour of full implementation of the ban, it recognised that there are other challenges pending in lower courts as well.

The San Francisco-based 9th Circuit Court of Appeals and the 4th US Circuit Court of Appeals in Richmond, Virginia, are both planning to hear arguments regarding the ban's legality this week. Those cases will then be heard by the Supreme Court.

What Has Happened to the Previous Travel Bans?

The ban that the Supreme Court upheld Monday is the third iteration of the policy that the President has authorised, and is the second to be green lit by the Supreme Court.

The very first of those bans was signed in the early days of the Trump presidency, and was quickly met with fierce opposition from protesters and lawyers upset by the chaotic scene that the hastily implemented ban had. Federal judges later blocked the ban, and the Trump administration later dropped that version of the ban altogether.

The second draft to the executive order was a bit smoother. Mr Trump signed the executive order in March, and gave advance warning for its implementation. Just before it was to go into effect, however, a federal judge blocked its implementation.

From there, the ban made its way to the Supreme Court, where the justices deferred to the administration and its claims that it requires leeway to keep the country safe.

The new version of the bill was drafted to be implemented after that ban expired.

What will the Supreme Court Decide when the Other Challenges Are Considered?

While it's impossible to say what the justices will ultimately decide, legal experts have said that their Monday ruling indicates that they are likely to rule in favour of the administration. The court has a long history of siding with the executive branch when it comes to measures concerning national security.

What Has the Reaction Been?

The Trump administration was predictably happy with the Supreme Court's decision, while civil rights groups expressed outrage.

US Attorney General Jeff Sessions said that the ruling was "a substantial victory for the safety and security of the American people." Meanwhile, White House spokesperson Hogan Gidley said the West Wing was "not surprised" by the decision.

The American Civil Liberties Union (ACLU) released a statement following the decision calling the President a bigot.

"President Trump's anti-Muslim prejudice is no secret—he has repeatedly confirmed it, including just last week on Twitter. It's unfortunate that the full ban can move forward for now, but this order does not address the merits of our claims. We continue to stand for freedom, equality, and for those who are unfairly being separated from their loved ones. We will be arguing Friday in the Fourth Circuit that the ban should ultimately be struck down," Omar Jadwat, the director of the ACLU's Immigrants' Rights Project, said.

Trump's Travel Ban Is Not Racist

Corine Gatti

"We are fighting an ideology and an ideology can't be fought with weapons."

In the following viewpoint, Corine Gatti argues against claims that a ban targeting predominantly Muslim countries is racist. She contends that doing so lumps all Muslims together. To make her case, the author quotes heavily from the Pakistani-Canadian journalist and activist Raheel Raza. Raza describes the important distinction between the faith of Islam and the violent politics of radical Islamism. Raza and the viewpoint author both argue that President Trump's travel ban can successfully prevent terrorism, thereby protecting both Muslims and non-Muslims. As Raza says, Muslims "need to choose which Islam" to follow. Gatti is an author with BeliefNet.com, a website dedicated to faith and inspiration.

AS YOU READ, CONSIDER THE FOLLOWING QUESTIONS:
1. How do Muslims feel about the travel ban, according to this viewpoint?
2. What does the author write is the difference between Islam as a religion and Islam as a political movement?
3. In what ways do Muslims suffer from Islamic terrorism, according to the viewpoint?

Individuals who visit or immigrate to another country are subject to the restrictions imposed by that country.

We've heard the travel ban issued by President Donald Trump riddled with many definitions. People called it a "Muslim ban," an "act of racism" and a "decision that erodes the fabric of America's liberties." Trump initially signed an executive order banning foreign nationals from Muslim-leading countries like Iraq, Iran, Libya, Somalia, Sudan, Syria and Yemen from entering the United States for 90 days until they were vetted. The updated list dropped Iraq and is still being fought in the courts. "Since 2001, hundreds of persons born abroad have been convicted of terrorism-related crimes in the United States," the White House said in a statement. "They have included not just persons who came here legally on visas but also individuals who first entered the country as refugees."

Raheel Raza is a Pakistani-Canadian journalist, author, anti-racism activist and works with the ClarionProject.org and is the President of Council for Muslims Facing Tomorrow. Both organizations educate the public about the dangers of radical Islam. The platforms are used for human rights activists to speak out against extremism and to work to find solutions. Raza agreed with the administration's assessment and as a devout Muslim, she supports tightening our borders and the US immigration laws.

"To address radicalization head-on is good for the future," she said after President Trump's first address to Congress about fighting radical Islamists. "We had the feeling that something was going to happen and of course, 9/11 came along and there were all these knee-jerk reactions and none of these were positive solutions to the problem. Many progressive Muslims decided that we need to have an open discussion on the problem," she explained. "Going into Iraq and Afghanistan never solved the problem. This is not a war of weapons. It is a war of ideas." We are fighting an ideology and an ideology can't be fought with weapons. Terrorism is the result of radicalization. "No one is born a terrorist. It's a human manifestation and the indoctrination of the minds of kids at a very young age. When they are indoctrinated in hate, they don't grow up to be normal 9 to 5 citizens with compassion and love in their hearts. The hate is then manipulated into violence," said the author of *Their Jihad ... Not My Jihad*.

The book examined how Muslims, their religion and their culture integrated into North American society, but there was and is an inner conflict. "The struggle of the soul is good enough and if we can become better human beings in our struggles, that is what our Jihad should be. We are not being taught that in institutions, we are taught that Jihad is justified. There are Muslims who fight this battle. There are Muslims who are speaking out and we need to do this together." Muslims have yet to successfully formulate an alternative to Islamism. There is a distinct difference from Islam as the spiritual faith and Islam as the continuation of the Abrahamic faith. "Islam compels me to follow the five basic foundational pillars of my faith, which is a form of worship. Then there is Islamism, which is political Islam, where Islam is politicized and becomes violent. We need to choose which Islam that we want to follow," she explained.

We asked if the travel ban was solely focused on Muslims. This is not against all Muslims, she corrected. "It's against Muslims who are distorting the faith. I realize that the anti-Trump movement is well-funded and very well planned. It doesn't matter what he says. I never believed that this was a ban against Muslims. As president of the United States, he could've banned Muslims from every country. But he hasn't and it is not permanent. We are speaking in a vacuum," she explained. She's right. After the travel ban was issued, there was a terror attack in London. A truck was driven into a crowd at a shopping center in central Stockholm, killing at least three people and injuring many others shortly after.

Strengthening the security of a nation is a president's job and right based on section 212(f) of the Immigration and Nationality Act of 1952: "Whenever the president finds that the entry of aliens or of any class of aliens into the United States would be detrimental to the interests of the United States, the president may, by proclamation, and for such period as he shall deem necessary, suspend the entry of all aliens or any class of aliens as immigrants or nonimmigrants or impose on the entry of aliens any restrictions he may deem to be appropriate."

President Barack Obama issued travel restrictions against Iraq in 2011 for six months after terrorists disguised themselves as refugees entered the country. President Bill Clinton and George W. Bush also issued bans. This is not about religion—the travel ban is to protect America. "You know, religion shouldn't come into it," said Raza. "It's a political move, the six countries are failed states, they have a lot of internal unrest. The rise of Jihad are in these states and they are unpredictable. It's a practical move by Trump in the right direction. Muslim leaders from other countries have supported Trump, but we never hear that in the news," she added.

This sends a strong message to other Muslim countries, who support, fund and train terrorists. "Unlike the previous president, this president is not going to be politically correct and will not stand for harm to come to his own country and this includes protecting Muslims. Terrorists have harmed and attacked Muslims more than they have non-Muslims."

EVALUATING THE AUTHOR'S ARGUMENTS:

Viewpoint author Corine Gatti quotes a Muslim activist who approves of the ban. How does this contribute to supporting the author's viewpoint? Review where the article's author quotes Raheel Raza, and where she inserts her own opinions. Is the resulting article neutral reporting or personal opinion?

Let's Not Pretend the Travel Ban Is About Fighting Terrorism

Kermit Roosevelt III

"It is hard to understand why the order selects the countries it does if the selection criterion is the degree of threat posed by foreign nationals."

Kermit Roosevelt III opens the following viewpoint by recalling a moment from history when refugees were turned away from America. He relates this incident from World War II to the events of today in order to prove that the United States isn't always as welcoming as the words engraved on the Statue of Liberty would suggest. Roosevelt then addresses the first version of President Trump's travel ban. He argues that there is little evidence that the travel ban would eliminate terrorism. Rather, he notes that business interests may be involved. His reasoning is that the ban avoids countries where the United States has strong economic ties or where Trump has business interests. The author also suggests the ban may go against the US Constitution. Roosevelt is a professor of constitutional law at the University of Pennsylvania Law School.

"Executive Order 13769: America at Its Best and Its Worst," by Kermit Roosevelt III, Foreign Policy Research Institute (FPRI) www.fpri.org,, February 1, 2017. Reprinted by permission.

AS YOU READ, CONSIDER THE FOLLOWING QUESTIONS:
1. How did Executive Order 13769 intend to affect the number of refugees to be admitted to America each year?
2. What three examples from history does the author use to explore Americans' reactions to immigrants and refugees?
3. How are Christians from the targeted countries treated by the travel ban?

The boat held 907 passengers, refugees fleeing war and religious persecution. Denied permission to land in the United States, it circled offshore while Coast Guard cutters prevented the captain from executing his last-ditch plan of grounding the vessel. After several days of fruitless negotiation, the ship turned away from America and back towards the refugees' home continent. They would eventually be accepted in various countries there, but that safety proved illusory: several hundred would still die as war and genocide overtook their new homes.

The boat was the German ocean liner *St. Louis*; the year was 1939. Despite Emma Lazarus' words on the Statute of Liberty welcoming the hungry, tired, and poor, the United States has a checkered history when it comes to accepting refugees. Still, President Trump's recent executive order 13769 stands out.

The stated purpose of the order is "to protect the American people from terrorist attacks by foreign nationals admitted to the United States." But as Ben Wittes argues, it is hard to understand the order as a good-faith attempt to pursue that goal. The order imposes a 90 day suspension on entry into the United States by persons from seven countries: Iran, Iraq, Libya, Somalia, Sudan, Syria, and Yemen. It suspends for 120 days the US Refugee Admissions Program, the means by which refugees are identified and admitted to the United States, with the stated intention of adding additional vetting procedures, excluding citizens of certain nations, and prioritizing claims of discrimination by religious minorities. It suspends indefinitely the entrance of Syrian refugees and caps the number of all refugees to be admitted in 2017 at 50,000. (The 2016 ceiling was 70,000.) Case by case exceptions are permitted.

Not everyone agreed that Trump's executive order was un-American. Many sided with the president in believing that security is of greater importance than freedom and acceptance.

At a quick look, the order bears some connection to terrorism. It's true that foreign nationals present in the United States have killed Americans. But which nationals? The 9/11 attacks were carried out by 15 Saudis, 2 men from the United Arab Emirates, and one each from Egypt and Lebanon. The 2002 shooter at Los Angeles International Airport was Egyptian. The 2013 Boston Marathon bombers were a Russian and a naturalized American. In San Bernardino in 2015, the attackers were one naturalized American and one Pakistani. There does not appear in recent history to have been a single American killed in the United States by a terrorist from any of the listed countries. It is hard to understand why the order selects the countries it does if the selection criterion is the degree of threat posed by foreign nationals.

Other criteria fit better with the order: it identifies predominantly Muslim countries with which the United States does not have a substantial economic relationship, and it omits countries where the Trump organization has business interests, according to Bloomberg. What it seems best calculated to do is

to inflict visible harm on Muslims regardless of the threat they pose while not compromising the economic interests of the United States or its president.

That is perhaps consistent with the preferences of some Trump supporters, and it is consistent with promises Trump made during the campaign. And there is certainly precedent for it in US history. People who feel threatened are reassured by hearing that their government has taken the gloves off; they are comforted by seeing it strike back against others who resemble the enemy, even if they are not in fact enemies. We saw this in the detention of Japanese Americans during World War II, in the embrace of torture after the September 11 attacks, in the invasion of Iraq. From this perspective, applying the entry ban to green card holders seeking to return to their families in the US is not a foolish overextension but a central feature: even these people, it says, will lose their rights for your safety; even your neighbors will be sacrificed for you. (There have been conflicting reports about the application of the ban to green card holders, but some have been detained and freed only by judicial order: two Iranian professors at the University of Massachusetts, for instance, were taken into custody at Logan airport after returning from an academic conference in Marseille.)

The order is likely not consistent, however, with federal law and the US Constitution. One provision of the Immigration and Naturalization Act, 8 U.S.C. section 1152, bans discrimination based on nationality in the issuance of immigrant visas. (Another gives the President the authority to exclude aliens he deems detrimental to American interests; the interaction of the two sections is unclear.) Green card holders have additional rights: when they leave the country and return they are generally not treated as aliens seeking admission and hence probably not subject to the President's authority to exclude such aliens. So US law may block some parts of the order.

The US Constitution may invalidate others. Several different constitutional arguments have been floated, but perhaps the strongest is that the order is motivated by impermissible religious bias—against Muslims and in favor of Christians. (The selection of the listed countries picks out Muslims; the preference for religious believers who are minorities in their countries of origin seems designed to pick out the Christians.) The order does not, of course, say this on its face, but statements by Trump surrogates and Trump himself, both during the campaign and in a recent interview with the Christian Broadcasting Network, suggest as much. The Due Process Clause of the Fifth Amendment, and both the Free Exercise and the Establishment Clauses of the First Amendment prohibit such discrimination.

We will find out. The order was, of course, immediately challenged in court. Judges around the country enjoined various parts of it while the cases proceeded. Acting Attorney General Sally Yates, expressing doubts about the order's legality, announced that the Department of Justice would not defend it. She was promptly fired, and her successor has reversed course.

Yates' defiance of the President was in some ways not entirely surprising: she was an Obama appointee marking time until Jeff Sessions is confirmed. But it highlights the disconnect between the Trump administration and the federal bureaucracy. There are conflicting reports as to whether the order was reviewed at all by the Office of Legal Counsel (OLC), which advises the executive branch and normally assesses orders before they are issued. Yates' letter seems to suggest that OLC reviewed the order, but it also uses an odd turn of phrase suggesting a circumscribed review: she noted that as Attorney General she needed to do more than OLC, which considered only whether the Order was "lawful on its face." This suggests that Yates believed that while the order did not facially constitute unlawful religious discrimination—since it does not mention any religions by name—other statements by, as she put it, the "administration or its surrogates" confirmed the unconstitutional purpose. (Georgetown law professor Marty Lederman elaborates on this argument here.)

Executive Order 13769 and the reaction to it show us America at its best and its worst. In its content, the order is pointlessly cruel. In its form it is amateurish: poorly-drafted, produced without consultation with the agencies charged with its enforcement and sprung upon them as a surprise. Even if it had been sensible, there were bound to be mistakes in implementation. In one, a five year old American boy was handcuffed and detained for hours, separated from his family. White House Press Secretary Sean Spicer, ignoring the American citizenship, justified the detention afterwards on the grounds that five-year old boys might well be security threats. "To assume that just because of someone's age and gender that they don't pose a threat," said Spicer, "would be misguided and wrong." In its letter announcing the firing of Sally Yates, the White House sounded like a five-year old itself. Yates was an "Obama administration appointee," the White House said, who had "betrayed the Department of Justice" and was "weak on borders and very weak on illegal immigration." All that was missing was the signature Trump epithet: loser. The Trump administration, thus far, is everything we feared: petty, vindictive, immature, incompetent, and unwilling to admit even its most obvious errors.

What we can be hopeful about is the response of the courts, which thus far have treated the challenges to the executive order with the seriousness they deserve, and of the American people, who have gone to airports to demonstrate their support for refugees. They show us a better understanding of America and its relation to the world, the understanding that hurting innocent people doesn't make us safer and shouldn't make us feel better. The Americans who went out to affirm that the lives of foreigners matter too were showing what is best about our country. Had there been such crowds on the beach in 1939, the death camps might have claimed several hundred fewer lives.

EVALUATING THE AUTHOR'S ARGUMENTS:

Viewpoint author Kermit Roosevelt III uses an example from history to start and end his article. How does this help him make his point? Would the article be stronger or weaker without these sections?

Trump's Travel Ban Makes Americans Less Safe

Ken Gude

"President Trump has further strained the already complicated relationship with Iraq and created a wedge between US troops and the allies and partners we need to fight IS."

In the following viewpoint, Ken Gude agrees with the previous author that the recent travel ban does not prevent terrorism. He additionally contends that the ban will make Americans less safe. Gude argues that the Islamic State will use the ban to disrupt the working relationship between US and Iraqi forces fighting terrorism in Iraq. The Islamic State, also known as IS, ISIL, or ISIS, is a militant organization that emerged in 2014 as an offshoot of al-Qaeda. This article was published on January 30, 2017, in response to the original proposed travel ban. The revised March version of the ban removed Iraq from the list of targeted countries. Gude is a senior fellow for national security at the Center for American Progress, a public policy research and advocacy group.

"Trump's Reckless Muslim Ban Makes Americans Less Safe," by Ken Gude, Center for American Progress, January 30, 2017. Reprinted by permission.

AS YOU READ, CONSIDER THE FOLLOWING QUESTIONS:
1. How would Trump's original travel ban have affected Iraqi citizens?
2. How did Iraq's Prime Minister respond to Trump's proposed travel ban?
3. How did the European leaders quoted respond to Trump's travel ban, according to the article?

President Donald Trump's Muslim ban not only has nothing to do with preventing terrorism, it also helps the Islamic State, or IS, and makes Americans less safe. According to data on terrorist attacks in the United States in the Global Terrorism Database compiled at the National Consortium for the Study of Terrorism and Responses to Terrorism at the University of Maryland, no American has ever been killed in a terrorist attack in the United States that has been carried out by a national of the now-banned countries. Since 1980, there have been 16 Islamist terrorist attacks in the United States that have killed Americans other than the perpetrator of the attacks. None of the perpetrators have been a national of the seven countries addressed in the ban: Iran, Iraq, Libya, Somalia, Sudan, Syria, or Yemen.

IS already is using the ban to drive a wedge between US and Iraqi forces fighting the terrorist group on the ground in Iraq. Outrage and condemnation have rained down on the United States since Trump signed the order Friday afternoon. Trump has only been president for a week and he is already isolating the United States, emboldening IS, and endangering Americans lives.

Trump's executive order stops all refugee resettlement for 120 days; suspends Syrian refugee resettlement indefinitely; and bars nationals from the seven banned countries from entering the United States for any reason for 90 days. This ban is inhumane, immoral, and a betrayal of American values. Slamming the door shut on refugees—the world's most vulnerable citizens who are fleeing unspeakable violence—is cowardly and makes America look weak not strong. It recalls the shameful episode in the 1930s when the United States refused to accept Jewish refugees fleeing Nazi persecution. Many of

Critics of the travel ban say it will not stop terrorism because the majority of terrorist acts on US soil, such as the deadly Pulse nightclub shooting in Orlando, Florida, are committed by American citizens who already live in the country.

those who were denied entry to the United States ended up being murdered by the Nazis. The refugees now barred by Trump's executive order may face similar fates.

The stated rationale of the ban is to prevent terrorists from entering the United States. Whatever Trump and his Republican allies may say, the ban will not accomplish this goal.

Even counting attacks that failed or were foiled during the execution of the plot, none were perpetrated by nationals of those seven countries. British citizen Richard Reid tried to detonate a bomb in his shoes onboard a US-bound airplane in 2002. Pakistani national Shahawar Matin Siraj and American James Elshafay were arrested in the later stages of planning to attack the New York City subway during the 2004 Republican National Convention. Afghan Najibullah Zazi was arrested when he too was plotting attacks on the New York City subway. Nigerian Abdul Farouk AbdulMutallab was prevented by alert passengers from detonating a bomb in his underwear. And Pakistani Faisal Shazad was arrested after his car bomb failed to detonate in New York City's Times Square.

In light of this data, it is hard to understand why the Trump administration chose these seven countries. Perhaps it is as cynical as the fact that the Trump Organization does not have any known business ties in those seven countries. Whatever the rationale, Trump's Muslim ban is already harming America's security interests.

Indeed, the executive order comes at a time when American troops continue to fight alongside Iraqi soldiers in the fight against IS. A high-ranking Iraqi general said Trump's order banning Iraqis from entering the United States "has caused massive disappointment in the hearts of every Iraqi who is fighting radicalism." Moreover, this executive order follows President Trump's repeated statements about taking Iraq's oil. Iraqi Prime Minister Haider al-Abadi, in response to these statements, has reassured his people that the oil is "the property of the Iraqis." By issuing this executive order, President Trump has further strained the already complicated relationship with Iraq and created a wedge between US troops and the allies and partners we need to fight IS. And IS is watching: Their propaganda channels are already pushing the line that the United States views Iraqi translators as "worthless."

Condemnation from key US allies has poured in since Trump signed the order late on Friday. British Foreign Secretary Boris Johnson called the move "divisive and wrong," and there is increasing pressure in the United Kingdom to cancel Trump's upcoming state visit. German Chancellor Angela Merkel's spokesperson said Merkel "regrets" the ban, and that fighting terrorism, "does not justify putting people of a specific background or faith under general suspicion." France's Foreign Minister Jean-Marc Ayrault said, "The reception of refugees fleeing the war, fleeing oppression, is part of our duties." Turkish Prime Minister Binali Yildirim said, "Regional issues cannot be solved by closing the doors on people."

Republican leaders, however, are lining up behind Trump's reckless action. Speaker of the House Paul Ryan said, "President Trump is right." Vice President Mike Pence and US Secretary of Defense James Mattis were both critical of the Muslim ban when it was proposed by Trump during the campaign, yet both were present when Trump signed the order Friday. They own this.

Trump's Muslim ban is destroying lives, causing untold damage to the security of the United States, and will not protect Americans from terrorist attacks. It must be withdrawn immediately.

EVALUATING THE AUTHOR'S ARGUMENTS:

Viewpoint author Ken Gude makes some of the same points as in the previous viewpoint. How does the tone differ between the two pieces of writing? How does this affect your response to the viewpoints, if at all?

Without Better Screening of Immigrants, We Need the Travel Ban

"The burden is on those who mean to show there is no evidence that nationals from the seven states have perpetrated acts of terror anywhere— like, for instance, in Europe."

Lee Smith

In the following excerpted viewpoint, Lee Smith argues in favor of President Trump's travel ban. The author claims that the countries in question do have the potential to send terrorists to the United States. He notes that Europe has a much larger number of refugees from countries such as Syria, and Europe has suffered from increasing terrorism. In addition, he suggests that the travel ban could prevent future attacks. He says that the countries in the travel ban are not targeted because of their predominant religion. Rather, they do not have proper screening processes that could help US immigration determine who might be a criminal or threat. Smith is a senior fellow at the Hudson Institute and former senior editor at the *Weekly Standard*, a conservative opinion magazine.

"Trump's Travel Ban Addressed Real Problems," by Lee Smith, This article was originally published in the *Weekly Standard*. http://www.weeklystandard.com, February 13, 2017. Reprinted by permission.

The unhappy reality is that the 9th Circuit Court's decision and much of the debate surrounding the executive order partake not of logic and reason but rather issue from a form of politicized hysteria and judicial arrogance.

The 9th Circuit Court argued that "The Government has pointed to no evidence that any alien from any of the countries [Iran, Iraq, Libya, Somalia, Sudan, Syria, Yemen] named in the Order has perpetrated a terrorist attack in the United States."

The language is precise but the intention is false. "Alien" refers to an individual who is not a US citizen, or US national, or permanent resident alien, also known as a green-card holder. In 2011, two Iraqi nationals admitted as refugees, i.e. "aliens," affiliated with al Qaeda and who fought against US troops in Iraq, were arrested in Bowling Green, Kentucky for plotting terrorist attacks in the United States, but did not manage to "perpetrate" one.

U.S dual-nationals, not aliens, from the seven states, as well as permanent resident aliens, have been involved in successful terrorist attacks and plots against the United States. Among others:

Abdul Razak Artan, a Somali refugee, and permanent resident alien, used his car and a knife to attack fellow students at the Ohio State University in December, 2016 before he was shot to death by police.

Anwar al-Awlaki was an American-born dual national with Yemeni citizenship who, according to Michael Leiter, former director of the National Counterterrorism Center, had a "direct operational role" in the "underwear bomber" plot against a Detroit-bound plane with 289 passengers aboard. Awlaki may also have played a part in the Fort Hood attack, which left 13 dead, and another 30 wounded.

President Trump's Travel Ban

US ban on citizens from 6 majority Muslim countries expires on Sept 24

President Trump's ban on individuals from majority Muslim countries from entering the United States was met with charges of discrimination.

Awlaki was killed in a 2011 drone attack ordered by President Barack Obama.

[...]

It's clear that nationals from the seven countries have waged, supported, or plotted terrorist attacks on American soil, but the point of the executive order isn't to punish for past incidents, or else Saudi Arabia, for instance, would be included on the list due to the number of Saudi nationals involved in the 9/11 attacks. The point rather is to protect against future attacks. The reason those seven countries are listed is because they are either state sponsors of terror (Iran, Sudan, Syria), or have dysfunctional central governments or none at all (Iraq, Libya, Somalia, Yemen), which make it more difficult to vet visa applicants with their home country.

Moreover, the United States has been involved in some form of armed conflict in all seven of these states over the last several years, which may put American interests in the crosshairs of various actors within these states, or of the states themselves.

Let's widen the focus some. As I say, the purpose of the executive order is not to punish but to prevent future attacks in the United States. To show that the executive order is a bad mistake, the burden is on those who mean to show there is no evidence that nationals from the seven states have perpetrated acts of terror anywhere—like, for instance, in Europe.

German authorities have stopped a number of terrorist attacks plotted by Syrian refugees affiliated with ISIS, including an attack on a major transportation hub. In July 2016, a Syrian refugee killed a woman with a machete near Stuttgart. The same month, a Syrian asylum seeker blew himself up at a musical festival, injuring 15 people.

Clearly the vast majority of Muslim refugees mean to escape violence, not carry it with them to Europe. But ISIS has used the refugee crisis to disguise their operators and seed European networks. According to a *Washington Post* report from April 2016, "over the past six months, more than three dozen suspected militants who impersonated migrants have been arrested or died while planning or carrying out acts of terrorism." Most notorious among them were members of the cell that waged multiple terrorist attacks in Paris in November 2015 that killed 137 and injured nearly 400.

[...]

And it's not just ISIS that's sending murderers to Europe among the refugees. Militiamen from Iranian-backed Iraqi Shia groups have relocated to the continent, as have war criminals who fought on behalf of Syrian despot Bashar al-Assad. Indeed, Iraq, Syria, and Iran have a long history of exploiting terror networks in Europe, especially in France. In other words, the problem is not simply that some bad people among the migrants are targeting Europe for terror attacks, but that Middle Eastern states are likely to infiltrate the refugee stream with operatives.

[...]

Was it a good idea for Europe to open its doors so widely to the problems that have turned the Middle East into a nightmare?

Is Europe a better, more diverse place for admitting the sociopathic murderers who fought to defend Assad? What is the upside of importing the region's issues, its wars and bloody conflicts? America has some portion of that experience. As former FBI director Robert Mueller told Congress in 2011 that among areas of "threat within the United States … relates to individuals going to Somalia to fight with al Shabab." Indeed there's a pipeline from Minnesota to Mogadishu that feeds the ranks of al Shabab, an al Qaeda affiliate, and now, NPR reported, ISIS.

There is no doubt that like the Somali community in Minnesota, the vast majority of Syrian asylum seekers, and visa applicants from the seven states listed, are decent and peaceful people who just want a chance to live, prosper, and raise their families outside a war zone. But the reason that America's experience of the refugee crisis is different from Europe's to date is largely because compared to the estimated one million-plus Syrian refugees now seeking asylum in Europe, America has received only a small fraction.

Since the Syrian conflict began in 2011, the United States has admitted around 15,000 refugees—a little more than 2,000 until 2016, when the Obama administration opened the doors to 12,500 Syrian refugees. Given the small number of refugees the United States has admitted as compared to how many Europe has, the burden of proof is on those seeking to show that Europe's experience is irrelevant to American national security.

Why wouldn't the odds of ISIS members or Assad militiamen sneaking into the United States increase as the number of refugees increases? The screening process is deeply flawed. As one former Obama administration official working on the refugee vetting process told the Washington Post, it's difficult to "determine something as basic as an applicant's criminal history." He continued: "We do the best with what we have… We talk to people about what their criminal histories are, and we hear about that. That's pretty much where we are."

[…]

After the Bowling Green case, US officials admitted to problems with a screening process that let through two Iraqi terrorists. "This case demonstrates specific gaps that were present in the screening process that was in place in the beginning of the [Obama] administration," one Department of Homeland Security Official told ABC News. "Once the administration became aware of these gaps, it took immediate steps to fill them. Today our vetting process considers a far broader range of information than it did in past years."

It's unfair to demand perfection from the agencies that protect American citizens, but they realize better than anyone that the vetting process is worse than imperfect. As FBI director James Comey told Congress in November 2015, "a number of people who were of serious concern" slipped through the screening of Iraq War refugees, including the two arrested on terrorism-related charges. "There's no doubt," said Comey, "that was the product of a less than excellent vetting."

The Iraqis were caught because their fingerprints matched those collected by American troops in Iraq. The United States doesn't have those capabilities in, say, Syria or Iran, nor do we have a relationship with the security services of those two State Department-designated state sponsors of terror that would allow American agencies to rely on the information they might provide. According to Comey, it's not going to get much better regarding Syrian refugees. "If we don't know much about somebody, there won't be anything in our data," the FBI director told Congress. "I can't sit here and offer anybody an absolute assurance that there's no risk associated with this."

That's an honest assessment from an honorable public servant. Unfortunately, much of the expert commentary of late is not. Consider, for instance, why many terrorism experts and former officials argue that the executive order won't help protect Americans at home. Some specialists, like Jessica Stern, tell us that in fact the executive order is "likely to make us less safe." The EO, said Paul Pillar, a former official at the CIA's Counterterrorism Center, "is not targeted at where the threat is, and the anti-Islam message that it sends is more likely to make America less safe." How does it make America less safe? Former CIA analyst Nada Bakos explains that, "All it does is help [Islamic State] recruiting." Yes, agrees ex-FBI agent Ali Soufan, "ISIS members and ISIS leaders, at least in their propaganda, have been calling President Trump and his ban and his recent policies a godsend."

That those experts and former officials opposed to the executive order contend that suspending visas to Syrian refugees indefinitely and temporarily suspending issuing visas to nationals from seven states will turn some Muslims into terrorists seems to me counterproductive reasoning, to say the least. There are only two logical conclusions to be drawn from this argument—either the United States should impose a permanent and total ban of Muslims until the region stops producing quantities of young men who will kill others if they don't get their way; or ISIS is entitled to a say in drafting America's national security and policies.

Both are absurd, and the latter is suicidal. For instance, Hezbollah and Hamas both have narratives, too, with Israel at the center of their paranoid and gruesome worldviews. Should the United States stiff-arm Israel so as not to play into the Hezbollah and Hamas narrative? What happens in the aftermath of a terror attack on America? Should we then tailor our policies to suit the demands of terrorists lest they strike again? How about if ISIS won't stop killing Americans until America admits numbers of refugees that are acceptable to ISIS?

You don't get it, say the experts. We're not trying to appease terrorists; we're making war on them and Trump's executive order is making it harder for us to work with regional partners, like the Iraqis. Fine, let the Iraqis throw out American troops. If the central government in Baghdad thinks it can tackle ISIS on its own, without American arms, training, special operations and air support, then we should pack up and go home. But they can't, which is why it would be self-defeating to stop working with the United States.

The United States is campaigning against ISIS in order to assist states either incapable of doing it themselves, or unwilling to. Further, it keeps the organization on the defensive in the region so that it doesn't wage attacks here at home. So, let's suppose that Trump has every intention of keeping his promise to wage a massive campaign against ISIS. In response, ISIS will do everything it can to stop that operation, and take revenge, by attacking targets in the American homeland. Will ISIS try to sneak its operatives into the refugee stream? Have they done so already? The answer to both questions, based on the group's behavior in Europe, is very likely. A Bataclan-like assault will be the least of it. Trump would be criminally irresponsible if he didn't do everything in his power to reduce the chances of that effort being successful.

[...]

Americans are entitled to an honest debate about immigration, the executive order, Syrian refugees, and how we might best balance our national security interests with humanitarian concern for the welfare of others as well as our wish to make our society better and stronger by welcoming those from around the world who share our most fundamental convictions as Americans. Would, for instance, those Syrian immigrants in flight from a mass murderer, and driven by industry, love of family, and love of their new country, make America a finer country? Do those Somali families whose sons go to Africa to wage war on behalf of an al Qaeda affiliate before returning to the Midwest make us a better nation?

We're owed that debate. We voted for that much at least. The courts have no legal right, no prerogative to take it from us.

EVALUATING THE AUTHOR'S ARGUMENTS:

In this viewpoint, Lee Smith claims that the countries listed in the travel ban do not supply clear, detailed, and accurate information about their citizens. Therefore US immigration cannot determine who is a potential terrorist. Does the author provide convincing information that this makes the travel ban necessary? How do his views compare to the viewpoints suggesting that the travel ban is racist?

Chapter 3

Who Deserves to Come to America?

What criteria determine who the United States welcomes past its borders?

President Trump Can't Hide the Racism at the Root of the Travel Ban

"The Trump administration's claims are as bogus now as they have been all along."

Nicole Colson

In the following viewpoint, Nicole Colson claims the Trump travel ban is rooted in bigotry (intolerance of those with other opinions) and xenophobia (fear and dislike of those from other countries). The author quotes from several political activists who are opposed to the travel ban. She also notes that two additional countries, which are not predominantly Muslim, are included in the later version of the ban. However, she argues that this later addition is merely an attempt to hide the fact that the ban is primarily targeting Muslims. Colson is a reporter for *Socialist Worker* newspaper and a contributor to the International Socialist Review and CounterPunch.

"Trump's new version of the same old racist ban," by Nicole Colson SocialistWorker.org, October 13, 2017. Reprinted by permission.

AS YOU READ, CONSIDER THE FOLLOWING QUESTIONS:
1. Did the third version of the travel ban impact Muslims more or less, according to the source cited in the article?
2. What two countries were given restrictions in the newer version of the ban?
3. How can activist protests affect the immigration ban, according to the article?

The Trump administration is back with a new anti-Muslim travel ban—and like the first two, this third version is rooted in bigotry and xenophobia. "Ban 3.0 has roughly the same grossly disproportionate impact on Muslims that Bans 1.0 and 2.0 had," Cornell law professor Michael Dorf wrote.

The latest travel ban actually affects more people than the original over time, and more severely. Instead of a 90-day ban (and a 120-day ban on refugees), Trump's latest order bars most travel from seven countries indefinitely, along with new restrictions on travel from two others.

As of October 18, most people wanting to travel from Iran, Libya, Syria, Yemen, Somalia, Chad and North Korea will be barred from entering the US, and some of those coming from Iraq or Venezuela will face additional security restrictions.

The ban applies in most cases to tourists, families of American residents and even people seeking medical visas—though Iranian students and those seeking business or tourist visas from Somalia may be allowed to enter the US if they receive extra screening.

People with permanent residency status are exempt, along with those who already have visas—but visa holders will not be allowed to renew them once they expire.

Trump's first travel ban, signed soon after he took office, was met with outrage and large, often spontaneous, demonstrations at airports across the country that brought out thousands to stand in defense of the rights of Muslims and refugees. That tidal wave of protest and public disgust pressured the courts for decisions that put the ban on hold.

Trump's hasty travel ban left travelers from the restricted countries in limbo, stuck in airports, and separated from their families.

The Trump administration came back with a slightly altered but equally racist ban in March that targeted six countries instead of seven—Iraq got left off the list—all of them with populations over 90 percent Muslim.

The second ban was also put on hold by multiple federal judges on the grounds that it clearly targeted all Muslims. A decision from the 4th US Circuit Court of Appeals stated in May that Trump's ban "drips with religious intolerance, animus and discrimination."

Enter the Supreme Court: In June, the high court lifted previous stays on the ban, allowing the most important sections to go into effect. The ban on travel from six countries as well as the entire US refugee program was upheld—but with an exception for those with "a credible claim of a bona fide relationship with a person or entity in the United States."

As Mukund Rathi wrote at SocialistWorker.org: "The Court's decision that the ban's supposed benefits to national security outweigh its possible harms is the height of imperial arrogance and cruelty: A message to people fleeing civil wars and sectarian bloodshed that have killed millions that their lives matter less than the remote chance than an American might be killed by a Muslim 'terrorist.'"

With the previous ban about to expire, the Trump administration rushed a new one into place, even before all the legal appeals of the last one were dealt with.

As Mariko Hirose, litigation director of the International Refugee Assistance Project (IRAP), said in a statement to Politico:

> *This case is certainly not moot for our clients and for all of those who continue to be discriminated against by this shameful order and its updated version. IRAP and our partners are not done fighting for the rights of refugees, Muslim Americans and their families. We will be back in court next week to challenge the most recent iteration of the Muslim ban. This administration should know that we will not give up until they're held accountable for their discriminatory actions.*

In theory, the new version of the ban will only remain in place until listed countries meet certain security requirements demanded by the Department of Homeland Security and prove they no longer have a "significant terrorist presence within their territory."

But meeting those standards will be difficult if not impossible, simply because of lack of technology in some cases.

There's also no clear understanding of what the latest ban will mean for those seeking to enter the US as refugees—the latest order doesn't apply to them.

However, the Trump administration signaled to Congress recently that it will cap the total number of refugees allowed into the US at 45,000 next year—the lowest number since 1980, when presidents first began setting a cap.

The cap was 110,000 during the last year of the Obama administration—and even that was woefully inadequate given the untold millions around the globe who have been forced to flee their homes as a direct result of US economic and military actions in the Middle East and beyond.

Now, the addition of North Korea and Venezuela to the list of targeted countries—though with limited restrictions, especially for Venezuela—reflects Trump's current political preoccupations with the hostile, nuclear-armed regime Kim Jong-un and the legacy of left-wing governments in Venezuela.

But there is another cynical purpose to the administration's action: Providing a possible legal counter to claims that the ban is unconstitutional because it discriminates on the basis of religion by primarily targeting Muslims.

In reality, there should be no doubt about the Islamophobia at the heart of the latest ban, any more than there was in previous versions. As Anthony Romero, executive director of the American Civil Liberties Union, said in a statement:

> *Six of President Trump's targeted countries are Muslim. The fact that Trump has added North Korea—with few visitors to the US—and a few government officials from Venezuela doesn't obfuscate the real fact that the administration's order is still a Muslim ban. President Trump's original sin of targeting Muslims cannot be cured by throwing other countries onto his enemies list.*

If version 3.0 of the travel ban was really about restricting entry of people from countries with a known terrorist presence, then it would include US allies like Saudi Arabia and Pakistan. The fact that the ban doesn't proves that the Trump administration's claims are as bogus now as they have been all along.

The indefinite time frame of this new action is especially troubling. "There is no light at the end of the tunnel anymore," Mirriam Seddiq, an immigration lawyer and founder of the American Muslim

Women Political Action Committee, told Vox. "Before, the argument was, 'This is only 90 days; why are you freaking out?'"

Likewise, the administration's decision to separate out the issue of refugees is likely an attempt to curtail popular anger—and the threat of a repeat of the kind of mass protests that hit airports when the first ban was announced.

At those protests, hundreds—and in some cases thousands—turned out to demand that refugees and others traveling to the US be allowed to enter. In some cases, lawyers and other immigrant rights advocates set up makeshift offices to help secure the release of vulnerable people caught in transit.

And in many cities, those first airport protests led directly to demonstrations of thousands more in the following days. It was one of the most inspiring examples of solidarity of the early days of the Trump presidency.

Now, as the latest ban gets set to take effect, activists are organizing a "No Muslim Ban Ever" day of action on October 18, sponsored by several immigrant rights groups. A return to the kind of protests we saw after the first ban will be necessary in the days and weeks ahead to halt this recycled version of Trump's racist policy.

EVALUATING THE AUTHOR'S ARGUMENTS:

In this viewpoint, Nicole Colson argues that every version of President Trump's travel ban is racist. She quotes several people to support her viewpoint. How does her choice of who to quote affect the article? Does it seem biased or unbiased?

Merit-Based Immigration Is Difficult to Judge

John Carson

> *"Merit can be an effective way to make choices, but also ... a powerful means of rationalizing biases and rendering them difficult to see."*

In the following viewpoint, John Carson explores the debate over who deserves to be an immigrant to the United States. Some people believe that immigration should be primarily reserved for people who are educated and speak English, because they will bring the most benefits to the United States. Others think that illegal immigrants who were brought to the United States as children should be allowed to stay. Yet other people think that refugees fleeing danger are the most deserving of protection. The author discusses the history of America in balancing "all men are created equal" with favoritism for certain groups. He claims that judging people based on merit is complicated and problematic. Carson is an associate professor of history at the University of Michigan.

AS YOU READ, CONSIDER THE FOLLOWING QUESTIONS:
1. What does "merit-based" immigration mean as the term was used by Donald Trump?
2. What is the danger of judging people based on merit, according to the author?
3. When can merit be hard to judge, according to the author?

F ierce debate over who deserves to be an immigrant to the United States has drawn on for decades.

Recently, President Donald Trump and hardliner Republicans have proposed overhauling the US immigration system to focus principally on "merit-based" immigration. As they define it, merit means being highly educated, fluent in English, relatively wealthy and having a job awaiting in the US.

Meanwhile, advocates of legal status for Dreamers—immigrants brought to the US as children without authorization—argue that these individuals are particularly deserving of protection, while refugee organizations underscore the dire situation of asylum seekers.

The lure of "merit" is clear: When choosing individuals for some reward, it may seem natural to prefer those who can claim to deserve it most. The concept of merit undergirds many aspects of everyday life: university admission practices, civil service hiring, police and firefighters' examinations, sports teams' tryouts and musical competitions.

However, as I discuss in my book "The Measure of Merit," rewarding the "best" has often helped justify treating people unequally. My research shows that ways of assessing merit are rarely neutral, and that questions of fairness arise when individuals or groups feel they have not received the same opportunities as others.

Equality and Merit

The use of merit to justify inequality has a long history in America. From the republic's founding, Thomas Jefferson's ringing declaration that "all men are created equal" was balanced against the widespread belief that some people, whether because of birth or education or

The United States no longer welcomes "the wretched refuse of your teeming shore." But maybe it never really did.

both, were more talented than others. These individuals, Jefferson and others argued, ought to be afforded greater opportunities, whether for advanced education or political leadership.

Jefferson celebrated the "natural aristocracy," and James Madison and Alexander Hamilton argued that indirect election of senators and the president would help ensure that only the most meritorious would rise to positions of political leadership. Merit, in fact, proved a powerful way of allowing one to embrace equality and yet still justify often profound differences in opportunity. Thus, at the nation's founding, women, African-Americans, Native Americans, noncitizen "aliens" and non-property-holding males were excluded from full political and civil rights.

Resistance was swift to the dominance of a privileged few, and slowly these basic rights were extended, first to white working-class males, then African-American men and finally women. However, there are still many circumstances where merit is employed as a way of unequally doling out limited resources. In these instances, it is crucial to ask two questions: Why turn to merit to choose some individuals over others, and how exactly will merit be gauged?

Complicating Merit

Merit is least controversial when the criteria for success are clear and the reward is appropriate. For example, few would protest that spots on the national Olympic track team go to the top finishers in an Olympic trial. There is only one measure of success—speed—and the Olympics seek a nation's best at that event.

Even in this case, however, some might question relying on a single trial rather than, say, all races run in the preceding six months or year. Merit can be tricky no matter how clear-cut the criteria.

When the task itself is complex, ranking performance becomes harder. There are also often real questions about whether small differences in performance matter beyond a certain level of proficiency.

For example, what attributes are required to be a good firefighter? Strength, speed, agility, courage, fortitude, intelligence—and the list could go on. So, should only the strongest or most courageous applicants be chosen? Or would choosing from a pool consisting of all those who are strong, fast, smart and brave enough to perform a firefighter's duties be better? Which approach will promote both competence and diversity? Merit can be an effective way to make choices, but also, as my book shows, a powerful means of rationalizing biases and rendering them difficult to see.

Immigration and Racial Exclusion

For almost a century, the United States had a relatively open immigration policy. Millions of Irish, Germans, Scots and Scandinavians, among others, emigrated to the US in the wake of economic upheavals and political repression in their home countries.

> **FAST FACT**
>
> In the United States, people can claim asylum if they can demonstrate a "well-founded fear of persecution" based on race, religion, nationality, political opinion, or membership in certain social groups.

However, starting in the 1880s, the government began to consider immigration restriction legislation, first with the Chinese Exclusion Act of 1882 and culminating in 1924 with the Immigration Act.

Merit was rarely explicitly mentioned as the rationale for preferring some groups over others. Nonetheless, the push to exclude Asians and then Eastern and Southern Europeans—mostly Catholics and Jews—echoed the period's ethnocentrism and infatuation with eugenics. Lawmakers viewed some "peoples"—primarily Northern Europeans—as biologically and culturally "superior." Restriction proponents argued that immigration should privilege these "superior" individuals.

Similarly, policymakers today must examine the use of merit to determine how it privileges certain groups and individuals at the expense of others.

What truly are the important attributes desired of a legal immigrant? Money? Advanced education? Good character? Willingness to do labor native-borns will not? Family ties?

How we answer depends on what goals we want to accomplish and values we wish to represent. Do we reward solely those who are already prospering? Or perhaps we should enact an immigration policy that also reflects the founding creed, that all people "are created equal."

EVALUATING THE AUTHOR'S ARGUMENTS:

Viewpoint author John Carson claims that rewarding individuals who've been identified as the "best" can justify treating people unequally. Do his examples support his claim? Why might it be challenging for politicians to determine who "deserves" to immigrate to their country?

America's Immigrants Deserve to Live with Their Families

"Family immigration is subject to significant limitations and it exists because American values include ideals such as family unification."

Raquel Aldana

In the following viewpoint, Raquel Aldana explains the concept of so-called "chain migration." This term refers to a process by which legal US residents or those holding a green card can sponsor a family member's immigration. The author notes that family immigration is limited in several ways, so it's not as easy or as open as its opponents suggest. She also notes that the United States does not have an especially high number of immigrants when considered as a percentage of the total US population. She goes on to argue that immigration benefits America and that the new standards for merit are unfair. Aldana is Associate Vice Chancellor for Academic Diversity and Professor of Law at the University of California, Davis.

"Debunking 3 myths behind 'chain migration' and 'low-skilled' immigrants," by Raquel Aldana, The Conversation, February 2, 2018, https://theconversation.com/debunking-3-myths-behind-chain-migration-and-low-skilled-immigrants-90787. Licensed under CC BY ND 4.0.

President Donald Trump has embraced the rhetoric of "chain migration" to spread the message that the United States is legally letting in too many of the wrong kind of immigrant. That term, however, distorts the facts.

As a scholar on US immigration law and policy, I'd like to correct and contextualize the numbers on the now maligned "family-based immigration," and uncover the biases that underlie the preference for the "highly-skilled" immigrant. Family immigration is subject to significant limitations and it exists because American values include ideals such as family unification.

Myth 1: Family Immigration Is Unlimited

On Jan. 5, the Trump administration published its framework on immigration reform and border security. To fulfill its promise to cut lawful immigration by half, the proposal limits family immigration to spouses and minor children of US citizens and lawful permanent residents. This proposed cut would eliminate the ability of US citizens and permanent residents to sponsor their siblings and adult children. It would also stop US citizens from sponsoring their parents.

To support these cuts, President Trump alleged in his first State of the Union address that current law creates a chain of migration that allows immigrants to sponsor "unlimited numbers of distant relatives." This claim is untrue.

With few exceptions, all lawful permanent immigration to the United States is subject to annual limits. Moreover, no single nation may send more than 7 percent of the overall total number of

Trump focused on the dangers of so-called chain migration, but experts say the practice occurs far less frequently than the president indicated.

immigrants coming to the United States in a given year. Only US citizens can sponsor immediate relatives—their spouses, minor and unmarried children and parents—without these limits. In recent years, immediate relatives have comprised nearly half of all family immigration to the United States.

All family immigration categories except immediate relatives are severely backlogged, and in particular for nations with high levels of immigration to the United States. In fact, applicants for family immigration from China, India, Mexico and the Philippines face wait times of up to 20 years. According to the US State Department, approximately 3.9 million immigrants are waiting in line for an opportunity to immigrate.

Myth 2: Family Immigration Is Overwhelming

The White House website features a chart on chain migration that presents a series of data points intended to suggest that legal immigrants are overwhelming the nation. For example, the chart states, "Every year the US resettles a population larger than the size of Washington DC." While factually correct, this data point distorts reality by ignoring context.

It's true that in absolute numbers, immigration to the United States is greater than any other country. However, it is small when considering the overall size of the US population. In fact, according to the libertarian CATO Institute, as a percentage of its population, US immigration flows rank relatively low as compared to other major industrialized nations such as Canada and Australia.

Myth 3: "Low-Skilled" Immigrants Don't Benefit US

The Trump administration has expressed a preference for highly skilled immigrants. The assumption is that immigration systems that value other factors—such as family unification, diversity or humanitarian goals—allows "low-skilled" immigrants into the US. They also assume these immigrants cannot or refuse to assimilate, or may even be dangerous. The profiles of permanent immigration to the United States today, however, reveal a much more positive reality.

Nearly 34 million legal permanent residents live in the United States, two-thirds of whom arrived based on family sponsorship. As a whole, demographic data show that lawful permanent residents work in a range of occupations and professions. They show good levels of social integration. Legal permanent residents and immigrants also generally have lower levels of criminality compared to the population of people born in the US.

Most studies on the fiscal impact of US immigration conclude that immigrant contributions have been positive to the overall US economy. They have little to no adverse impact on native workers.

There are, however, variations among immigrants across measures such as educational attainment, home ownership and English proficiency. In general, for example, Asian immigrants outperform immigrants from Latin American and even the native born on some of these measures. But there are historical and geographic reasons that explain why immigrants from Mexico and Central America to the United States have tended to be from poorer and more vulnerable communities.

These variations do not mean that some immigrants integrate poorly or fail to contribute to US society. Rather, their contributions are devalued in this new rhetoric of "merit" migration.

This new standard of "merit"—measured in terms of high levels training and education, English-language proficiency and high wages—creates a hardly achievable race to the top. It narrows the definition of who should be considered a "deserving" immigrant. Nearly all US citizens would likely be undeserving of US immigration under these standards.

Other important values are lost that I believe should continue to define our identity as a nation. These values include family unification, compassion toward people who are persecuted and being good neighbors. They also mean valuing the contributions of immigrants who do the difficult work of picking our fruit, cleaning our houses, cutting our lawns and caring for our children and elderly.

EVALUATING THE AUTHOR'S ARGUMENTS:

Viewpoint author Raquel Aldana argues against immigration based on a new standard of merit. Compare her points to those in the previous viewpoint, which also argues against merit-based standards. How do the two articles differ in their approach? Does one or the other present a stronger argument? If so, how?

International Students Benefit America

> "*Domestic and international student integration on American university campuses is ... important for the future of national and economic security.*"

Paula Calligiuri

In the following viewpoint, Paula Calligiuri argues that President Trump's travel restrictions are causing fewer international students to apply to US colleges and universities. The author asserts that international students are a benefit to America. For one, they help US students achieve a "cultural agility" that makes them more suited for domestic and international jobs. Meanwhile, foreign students who study in the United States and return to their home countries help their neighbors see America in a better light. Therefore, in the author's view, US immigration policy should be encouraging more international students to come to the United States, not fewer. Calligiuri is the Director of the Center for Human Resource Strategy at Rutgers University.

AS YOU READ, CONSIDER THE FOLLOWING QUESTIONS:
1. Why are fewer international students applying to US universities, according to the article?
2. What are the advantages to having international students study in the United States, according to the sources cited?
3. What is "cultural agility"?

The Trump administration's nationalism (as most recently witnessed in his pro-travel ban Twitter reaction to the London attacks) has had an unfortunate effect on universities in the United States. Namely, some international students, surmising that they're unwelcome or unsafe studying in the US, are not applying. As a result, many American universities are reporting a significant decline in international student applications.

This decline in applications, while applauded by those hoping to improve admissions for American students, has unintended long-term consequences: It makes America less safe and less prepared for future global growth.

As a researcher studying how individuals develop cross-cultural competencies, I've found that domestic and international student integration on American university campuses is essential for building cultural understanding—important for the future of national and economic security.

The Need for Student Integration

Over 600 university presidents recently reminded Secretary of Homeland Security John Kelly of international students' benefit to national security. In a letter dated Feb. 3, 2017, they stated that international students who study in the United States return to their home countries as "…ambassadors for American values, democracy and the free market."

According to NAFSA (a nonprofit organization for international educators), international students can help to counteract negative stereotypes of Americans back in their home countries. Research has found that college students with friends from different countries are

Travel bans impede the ability of international students to live and study in the United States. This not only has a detrimental effect on the students and their peers, but it also hurts universities.

more open-minded and had less apprehension when engaging in conversation with people from different countries. Both, I believe, are useful characteristics to combat terrorism; those who like Americans would seem less likely to attack America.

In addition to the benefit for national security, integration of international students is critical for American students' development of cultural agility: the ability to work comfortably and effectively in different countries and with people from different cultures. Cultural agility is a competency in high demand by employers, making it an asset for both American and international students upon graduation.

Roughly one-third of multinational firms cite a lack of culturally agile employees as a limit to their global competitiveness. When over 13,000 professionals from 48 countries rated their effectiveness on 12 managerial tasks, the three tasks with the lowest ratings were those with an intercultural component: integrating oneself into foreign environments, intercultural communication, and leading across countries and cultures. Clearly, it's a skill valued by employers, but lacking in the workforce.

My research has found that cultural agility can be readily fostered on diverse college campuses that successfully promote inclusion. It is gained over time, through collaboration and friendship among those from different cultures.

Fostering International and Domestic Student Integration

Some universities have started #YouAreWelcomeHere campaigns to attract international students with a countervailing message of openness and inclusion. The campaign will, hopefully, also encourage wary international students to apply. Enrollment, however, is only half the solution. What happens when the international students arrive?

While studying in another country holds promise for developing cross-cultural competencies, the reality is all too often quite different. According to the South China Morning Post, 25 percent of Chinese students attending Ivy League universities in the US dropped out of school. Many reported difficulties adjusting to the new environment.

For those international students who do not drop out, nearly 40 percent of them reported having no close American friends but would like to have more meaningful relationships, based on a study of over 450 international students attending 10 public universities in the United States. International student experiences fall short of the expectation that cross-cultural bonding and skill-building will occur automatically; sharing a campus and classes is not enough to form friendships.

College is a stressful period. When under periods of stress, students, like all of us, have the greatest cognitive and emotional comfort with those who they perceive are going through the same experience.

The result is that people from the same country, when placed in a new country together as foreigners, connect with one another. We see this when we walk around not only college campuses but also expatriate communities abroad. While it is a natural human response, students who associate only with other similar students miss the opportunity to develop their cultural agility.

In an intervention piloted at the College of Business Administration at Kent State University, we found that student integration could be fostered by training both international and domestic students in conversational and cultural skills. The study, while not yet published, found that students who participated in this skill-building program had greater openness and higher levels of integration when compared to a control group. The benefit was an increased sense of ease to make friends on campus, better perceptions of social support, a sense of belonging and overall satisfaction, especially among those students who were less open when starting their freshman year.

Looking Ahead

Students, both international and domestic, benefit from their multicultural friendships. Through their college friendships, they can demystify differences and become more open to people from different countries and cultures. This ease with cultural difference is the foundation of cultural agility.

This cultural agility can, in turn, have a lasting, positive effect on their personal career success and international cooperation.

The challenge, especially in today's environment, is for universities to get ahead of the decline in international student applications before it becomes a detrimental trend. If not addressed, the opportunities for cultural development will be limited, potentially eroding national security and our students' professional success as they compete in the global economy.

Fear of "The Other" Leads to Increases in Hate Crimes

"Muslims are also easy targets for a new generation of nativists, whose fears are used to justify turning away refugees and immigrants."

Ingrid Anderson

The following viewpoint addresses a rise in anti-Semitism, prejudice against Jewish people. Ingrid Anderson argues that this and other forms of hate crimes were on the rise at college campuses and elsewhere during and after the 2016 presidential election. She compares this to the political climate between the first and second world wars. In both cases anti-immigrant and anti-Semitic feelings increased. The author argues that these feelings are due to fear rather than a rational understanding of immigration. Anderson is a lecturer in the Arts & Sciences Writing Program at Boston University.

AS YOU READ, CONSIDER THE FOLLOWING QUESTIONS:

1. What are nativists and how did they affect earlier US immigration policies?
2. How are the attitudes toward immigrants today similar to those of the interwar period?
3. How did Trump supporters' views of immigration differ from those of Hillary Clinton's supporters, at the time this viewpoint was written?

This poster, which reads "We the People Are Greater Than Fear," is part of a series depicting Muslim, Latina, and African American women. It was designed to remind the public of America's values.

This February, more than 100 gravestones were vandalized at the Chesed Shel Emeth Society Cemetery outside of St. Louis, Missouri and at the Jewish Mount Carmel Cemetery in Philadelphia.

The Anti-Defamation League (ADL) has called anti-Semitism in the US a "very serious concern." An ADL task force confirmed that 800 journalists in the US have been targeted with more than 19,000 anti-Semitic tweets. The organization also reported an upsurge in anti-Semitism on US college campuses.

Most disconcerting, however, is the ADL's admission that, although this increase in anti-Semitism is troubling, "it is essential to recognize that, for both positive and negative reasons—we are not alone." In the 10 days following the presidential election in 2016, nearly 900 hate-motivated incidents were reported, and many on college campuses. Many of these incidents targeted Muslims, people of color and immigrants as well as Jews.

White supremacist groups like Identity Evropa, American Vanguard and American Renaissance have also been more active on college campuses.

I am a Jewish studies scholar. Research shows that this out-pouring of anti-immigrant and anti-Semitic sentiment is reminiscent in many ways of the political climate during the years between the first and second world wars in the US—known as the interwar period.

FAST FACT

It is difficult to determine whether immigrants are more or less often criminals than US citizens are. Depending on the data used and how it is interpreted, a case may be made that noncitizens are more criminal than citizens—or that they are far less criminal.

America as the "Melting Pot"

In its early years the United States maintained an "open door policy" that drew millions of immigrants from all religions to enter the country, including Jews. Between 1820 and 1880, over nine million immigrants entered America. By the early 1880s, American nativists—people who believed that the "genetic stock" of Northern Europe was superior to that of Southern and Eastern Europe—began pushing for the exclusion of "foreigners," whom they "viewed with deep suspicion."

In fact, according to scholar Barbara Bailin, most of the immigrants, who were from Southern, Central and Eastern Europe, "were considered so different in composition, religion, and culture from earlier immigrants as to trigger a xenophobic reaction that served to generate more restrictive immigration laws."

In August 1882, Congress responded to increasing concerns about America's "open door" policy and passed the Immigration Act of 1882, which included a provision denying entry to "any convict, lunatic, idiot or any person unable to take care of himself without becoming a public charge."

However, enforcement was not strict, in part because immigration officers working at the points of entry were expected to implement these restrictions as they saw fit. In fact, it was during the late 19th century that the American "melting pot" was born: nearly 22 million immigrants from all over the world entered the US between 1881 and 1914. They included approximately 1,500,000 million European Jews hoping to escape the longstanding legally enforced anti-Semitism of many parts of the European continent, which limited where Jews could live, what kinds of universities they could attend and what kinds of professions they could hold.

Fear of Jews/Immigrants

Nativists continued to rail against the demographic shifts created by the United States' lax immigration policy, and in particular took issue with the high numbers of Jews and Southern Italians entering the country, groups many nativists believed were racially inferior to Northern and Western Europeans. Nativists also voiced concerns about the effects of cheaper labor on the struggle for higher wages.

These fears were eventually reflected in the makeup of Congress, since the electorate voted increasing numbers of nativist congresspeople into office who vowed to change immigration laws with their constituent's anti-immigrant sentiments in mind.

Nativist and isolationist sentiment in America only increased, as Europe fell headlong into World War I, "the war to end all wars." On Feb. 4, 1917 Congress passed the Immigration Act of 1917, which reversed America's open door policy and denied entry to the majority of immigrants seeking entry. As a result, between 1918 and 1921, only 20,019 Jews were admitted into the US.

The 1924 Immigration Act tightened the borders further. It transferred the decision to admit or deny immigrants from the immigration officers at the port of entry to the Foreign Services Office, which issued visas after the completion of a lengthy application with supporting documentation.

The quotas established by the act also set strict limits on the number of new immigrants allowed after 1924. The number of Central and Eastern Europeans allowed to enter the US was dramatically reduced: The 1924 quotas provided visas to a mere 2 percent of each nationality already in the U.S by 1890, and excluded immigrants from Asia completely (except for immigrants from Japan and the Phillipines). The stated fundamental purpose of this immigration act was to preserve the ideal of US "homogeneity." Congress did not revise the act until 1952.

Why Does this History Matter?

The political climate of the interwar period has many similarities with the anti-immigrant and anti-Semitic environment today.

President Trump's platform is comprised in large part of strongly anti-immigrant rhetoric. A Pew Charitable Trust survey shows that as many as 66 percent of registered voters who supported Trump consider immigration a "very big problem," while only 17 percent of Hillary Clinton's supporters said the same. Seventy-nine percent of Trump supporters embrace the proposal to build a wall "along the entire US border with Mexico." Moreover, 59 percent of Trump supporters actively associate "unauthorized immigrants with serious criminal behavior."

I argue that much like the claims of interwar period nativists that Southern and Eastern European people were racially inferior, the assertions of President Trump and his supporters about immigrants and the dangers they pose are nothing more than demagoguery. The allegations about the high crime rate among immigrants are not borne out by statistical evidence: Immigrants are far less likely to commit crimes than people born in the US.

President Trump's claims about the dangers posed by immigrants may not be supported by facts; but they do indicate the US' increased isolationism, nativism and right-wing nationalism. His most recent travel ban blocks immigrants from six predominantly Muslim nations, and includes a 120-day freeze on Syrian refugees specifically. And yet like the Jews of Europe from the interwar period, many of these refugees seek entry into the US because their very lives are at stake.

For many scholars like myself, Trump's "America First" approach is a reminder of the interwar period; all over again, we see anti-immigrant sentiment and anti-Semitism, going hand in hand. In the current climate, Muslims are also easy targets for a new generation of nativists, whose fears are used to justify turning away refugees and immigrants.

EVALUATING THE AUTHOR'S ARGUMENTS:

In this viewpoint, author Ingrid Anderson argues that anti-immigrant feelings are due to unreasonable fears. How does Anderson support her claims? Do you agree with her comparison of current feelings and the interwar period?

Editor's note: These facts can be used in reports to add credibility when making important points or claims.

Immigration Terms

- *Immigration* refers to the act of coming to a foreign country to live permanently. This can happen with or without legal authorization. The term *alien* is used to refer to a foreigner, especially one who is living in a country where they are not a citizen. It is sometimes viewed as a derogatory term. In immigration terms, a *citizen* is a legally recognized member of a nation. They may be a citizen by birth, or they may be *naturalized*, having gone through a process to become a legal citizen.

- A *refugee* is a person who has fled their country because of war, violence, natural disaster, or persecution. The number of refugees allowed into the United States each year has varied greatly. In the fiscal year ending in September 2016, the US admitted 84,995 refugees. The Democratic Republic of the Congo accounted for the most refugees at 16,370. The next highest numbers were Syria (12,587), Burma (also known as Myanmar, 12,347), Iraq (9,880), and Somalia (9,020). Of total refugees that year, 46 percent identified as Muslim and 44 percent identified as Christian.

- In border control terms, *travel* refers to shorter, temporary stays in a foreign country. Throughout the world, most countries place restrictions on both immigration and travel. Laws can limit who is allowed to enter a country, under what circumstances, and how long they may stay. The rules can also require specific documents such as passports and visas.

Border Control in the United States

- The first law concerned with allowing foreigners to become US citizens was the Naturalization Act of 1790. This statute said that white males could become citizens if they were not indentured (bound as an apprentice or laborer). They first had to live in the United States for two years. At that time, only free white males could be citizens.
- The US Border Patrol was created in 1924 and expanded in 1996. According to US Customs and Border Protection, "The priority mission of the Border Patrol is preventing terrorists and terrorists weapons, including weapons of mass destruction, from entering the United States."
- An Office of Homeland Security was created in 2001, eleven days after the September 11 terrorist attacks. The Department of Homeland Security (DHS) came into being after an Act passed by Congress in November 2002. It integrated all or part of twenty-two different federal departments and agencies. The DHS is charged with safeguarding the American people. This includes preventing terrorism, enhancing security, managing the country's borders, administering immigration laws, and preparing for disasters.
- The US Government Accountability Office has reported on terrorist attacks in the United States. The 9/11 attacks had the largest number of deaths, with nearly three thousand people killed. Between September 12, 2001 and December 31, 2016, eighty-five attacks by violent extremists resulted in 225 deaths. Of those, radical Islamist violent extremists committed twenty-three separate attacks and killed 119 people. Far-right violent extremists (such as white supremacists) committed sixty-two separate attacks and killed 106 people.

Who Gets In

- In the United States, people have been prohibited from visiting or immigrating for a variety of reasons. At certain times they could be banned if they had a contagious disease, were homosexual, or were considered physically or mentally "unfit." People have also been banned for certain political views, criminal convictions, and association with terrorist organizations. The specifics change with time.

- One clause in the US Code seems to give the president the authority to ban anyone from the country, for any reason. However, this clause may contradict other US laws and even the Constitution.

Executive Orders 13769 and 13780

- On January 27, 2017, President Trump signed Executive Order 13769. This rule attempted to prevent people from seven countries from entering the United States: Iraq, Syria, Iran, Yemen, Sudan, Somalia, and Libya.
- According to the US Department of Homeland Security, "The Executive Order signed on January 27, 2017 allows for the proper review and establishment of standards to prevent terrorist or criminal infiltration by foreign nationals…. In order to ensure that the United States government can conduct a thorough and comprehensive analysis of the national security risks posed from our immigration system, it imposes a 90-day suspension on entry to the United States of nationals of certain designated countries…." This Executive Order also banned Syrian refugees indefinitely. It capped the number of all refugees to be admitted in 2017 at 50,000, which was lower than in recent prior years.
- The countries listed in the original travel ban all had populations that were primarily Muslim. For this reason, the ban was sometimes referred to as a "Muslim ban." The Executive Order faced legal challenges in many states and was blocked by federal courts.
- On March 6, 2017, President Trump issued Executive Order 13780. This was titled Protecting The Nation From Foreign Terrorist Entry Into The United States. This revised ban removed Iraq from the list of countries, although it called for "additional scrutiny" for Iraqis. The indefinite ban on Syrian

refugees became a limited-time ban. The new ban no longer applied to permanent US residents.

- Once again the Order faced court challenges. In June 2017, the Supreme Court allowed the March version of the President's Executive Order to take partial effect. The Court allowed entry to "foreign nationals who have a credible claim of a bona fide relationship with a person or entity in the United States." The Court specified that this would include foreign college students. However, some educators and legal experts still warned that international students might have trouble with visas. Legal challenges to Executive Order 13780 continued in lower state courts.

- President Trump won the 2016 election partly by promising stronger laws against legal and illegal immigration. Many of his supporters agreed with his claims that illegal immigrants bring serious crime to the United States. It is difficult to determine whether immigrants are more or less often criminals than US citizens are. The numbers change depending on the data used and the methods used to interpret them. The total immigrant population of the country is about 13.5 percent. In federal prisons, 11 to 20 percent of the total prison population are noncitizens. Some of these prisoners were arrested for immigration violations. Meanwhile, 90 percent of incarcerated people in the United States are in state and local prisons or jails. There, noncitizens made up 4 percent of the total prison population. A case may be made that noncitizens are more criminal than citizens—or that they are far less criminal. It all depends on the data used and how it is interpreted.

Organizations to Contact

The editors have compiled the following list of organizations concerned with the issues debated in this book. The descriptions are derived from materials provided by the organizations. All have publications or information available for interested readers. The list was compiled on the date of publication of the present volume; the information provided here may change. Be aware that many organizations take several weeks or longer to respond to inquiries, so allow as much time as possible for the receipt of requested materials.

American Civil Liberties Union (ACLU)
125 Broad Street, 18th Floor
New York, NY 10004
(212) 549-2500
contact form: www.aclu.org/general-feedback
website: www.aclu.org
The ACLU works to defend and preserve the individual rights and liberties guaranteed by the Constitution and laws of the United States. The ACLU Immigrants' Rights Project is dedicated to expanding and enforcing the civil liberties and civil rights of immigrants.

American Friends Service Committee (AFSC)
1501 Cherry Street
Philadelphia, PA 19102
(215) 241-7000
contact form: www.afsc.org/contact
website: www.afsc.org
AFSC is a Quaker organization devoted to service, development, and peace programs throughout the world. A key issue is defending immigrant rights.

American Immigration Council
1331 G Street NW, Suite 200
Washington, DC 20005
(202) 507-7500
contact form: www.americanimmigrationcouncil.org/contact-us
website: www.americanimmigrationcouncil.org
This nonprofit organization promotes laws, policies, and attitudes that support immigration and help immigrants stand up for their rights. The website offers information about the positive impact of immigrants and ways to get involved.

The Brookings Institution
1775 Massachusetts Avenue NW
Washington, DC 20036
(202) 797-6000
email: communications@brookings.edu
website: www.brookings.edu
The Brookings Institution is a nonprofit public policy group. Its mission is to conduct in-depth research that leads to new ideas for solving the problems facing society at the local, national, and global level.

The Essential Worker Immigration Coalition (EWIC)
2101 L Street, NW, Suite 1000
Washington, DC 20037
(703) 749-1372
website: http://ewic.org
EWIC is a coalition of national businesses and trade associations that support immigration reform. It is concerned with the shortage of both semi-skilled and unskilled labor. EWIC supports policies that facilitate the employment of essential workers by US companies that are unable to find American workers.

The Heritage Foundation
214 Massachusetts Ave NE
Washington, DC 20002-4999
(202) 546-4400
email: info@heritage.org

website: www.heritage.org
The Heritage Foundation is a conservative research center. Its goal is to effectively communicate conservative policy research to Congress and the American people. Issues include immigration and terrorism.

Immigrant Legal Resource Center (ILRC)

1663 Mission Street, Suite 602
San Francisco, CA 94103
(415) 255-9499
email: lmogannam@ilrc.org
website: www.ilrc.org
The ILRC works with and educates immigrants, community organizations, and the legal sector. Its mission is to build a democratic society that values diversity and the rights of all people. The ILRC publishes expert immigration practice manuals used by legal services providers.

Immigration Voice

1177 Branham Lane #321
San Jose, CA 95118
(202) 386-6250
email: info@immigrationvoice.org
website: immigrationvoice.org
Immigration Voice is a national nonprofit organization working to alleviate the problems faced by legal high-skilled immigrants. They act as an interface between these immigrants and the legislative and executive branches of the government.

Migration Policy Institute (MPI)

1400 16th Street NW, Suite 300
Washington, DC 20036
(202) 266-1940
email: Info@MigrationPolicy.org
website: www.migrationpolicy.org
MPI provides analysis and evaluation of migration and refugee policies. Its guiding philosophy is that international migration needs active and intelligent management. MPI publishes an online journal.

For Further Reading

Books

Bauman, Zygmunt. *Strangers at Our Door*. Cambridge, UK: Polity, 2016.

A look at the origins and impact of Americans' panic over immigration. The author shows how politicians have exploited fears and anxieties, and he explores new ways to live together.

Chomsky, Aviva. *They Take Our Jobs!: And 20 Other Myths about Immigration*. Boston, MA: Beacon Press, 2007.

A look at immigration myths that affect how most people think about immigration.

Chomsky, Aviva. *Undocumented: How Immigration Became Illegal*. Boston, MA: Beacon Press, 2014.

This book explores what it means to be undocumented in a legal, social, economic, and historical context.

Daniels, Roger. *Coming to America: A History of Immigration and Ethnicity in American Life*. New York, NY: Harper Perennial, 2002.

A study of immigration to the United States from the colonial era to the present.

Daniels, Roger. *Guarding the Golden Door: American Immigration Policy and Immigrants since 1882*. New York, NY: Hill and Wang, 2005.

A history of US immigration, focusing on the politics behind immigration law.

Execvisa. *Visas for the United States: Execvisa*. Execvisa, 2015.

A guide to the many types of visas that allow people to work and do business legally in the United States.

Gerber, David A. *American Immigration: A Very Short Introduction*. Oxford, UK: Oxford University Press, 2011.

A look at immigration and anti-immigration feelings in US history. The author examines the many legal efforts to curb immigration and to define who is and is not an American.

Hoyt, Joanna Michal. *A Wary Welcome: The History of U.S. Attitudes toward Immigration*. Independently published, 2017.

A history of American immigrants and American responses to immigration.

Olsen, Laurie. *Made in America: Immigrant Students in Our Public Schools*. The New Press, 2008.

This book studies a public high school where more than 20 percent of students were born in another country. The author explores issues such as bilingual education through interviews with teachers, students, and parents.

Periodicals and Internet Sources

ACE, Higher Education Groups Say Trump Travel Ban Threatens Colleges' Ability to Attract International Students, Scholars," American Council on Education, September 19, 2017. http://www.acenet.edu/news-room/Pages/Trump-Travel-Ban-Threatens-Colleges-Ability-to-Attract-International-Students-Scholars.aspx.

Carapezza, Kirk, "Travel Ban's 'Chilling Effect' Could Cost Universities Hundreds of Millions," NPR, April 7, 2017. https://www.npr.org/sections/ed/2017/04/07/522773429/travel-bans-chilling-effect-could-cost-universities-hundreds-of-millions.

"Federal Register Notice: Criteria for Recommending Federal Travel Restrictions for Public Health Purposes, Including for Viral Hemorrhagic Fevers," Centers for Disease Control and Prevention. https://www.cdc.gov/quarantine/criteria-for-recommending-federal-travel-restrictions.html.

Fields, Amanda, "Travel Ban Necessary for American Security," *The Collegiate Times*, February 21, 2017. http://www.collegiatetimes.com/opinion/travel-ban-necessary-for-american-security/article_cd4b5fec-f88c-11e6-af48-77b611d87824.html.

Friedman Valenta, Jiri and Leni, and Jim Arkedis, "Pro & Con: Immigration Ban: Has Trump Begun to Destroy or to Defend America?" *Mishpacha*, February 01, 2017. http://www.mishpacha.com/Browse/Article/7193/Pro—Con-Immigration-Ban.

Gerstein, Josh, "5 Questions on the Future of Trump's Travel Ban," *Politico*, June 26, 2017. https://www.politico.com/story/2017/06/26/supreme-court-trump-travel-ban-239970.

Greene, Alan, "Trump's travel ban is nothing to do with national security," *The Conversation*, February 2, 2017. https://theconversation.com/trumps-travel-ban-is-nothing-to-do-with-national-security-72170.

Hargrove, John W. "Trump's Travel Ban Survives Latest Trip to the Supreme Court," *Labor & Employment Insights*, December 7, 2017. https://www.employmentlawinsights.com/2017/12/trumps-travel-ban-survives-latest-trip-to-the-supreme-court/.

Kertscher, Tom, "Is Donald Trump's Executive Order a 'Muslim Ban'?" *Politifact*, February 3rd, 2017. http://www.politifact.com/wisconsin/article/2017/feb/03/donald-trumps-executive-order-muslim-ban/.

Komar, Emma, and Megan Munce, "Sanctuary Cities: Pro or Con?" *The Voice*, May 22, 2017. http://presentationvoice.com/all-posts/news/2017/05/22/sanctuary-cities-pro-or-con/.

Lonergan, Brian, "Travel Ban Illustrates the Danger of Treating National Security as Political Football," *The Hill*, October 28, 2017. http://thehill.com/opinion/immigration/357653-travel-ban-illustrates-the-danger-of-treating-national-security-as.

Mitchell, Andrea, and Richie Duchon, "Trump Travel Ban Makes America Less Safe: Ex-Top Security, State Officials," NBC News, February 6, 2017. https://www.nbcnews.com/news/us-news/trump-travel-ban-makes-america-less-safe-ex-top-security-n717206.

Narula, Svati Kirsten, "Trump Ordered a US Intelligence Report to Justify His Travel Ban. This Is What He Got Instead," *Quartz*, February 25, 2017. https://qz.com/919257/department-of-homeland-security-report-rejects-donald-trumps-travel-ban-claims/.

"New Travel Restrictions Replacing Trump's Travel Ban," Center for Security Policy, September 26, 2017. https://www.centerforsecuritypolicy.org/2017/09/26/new-travel-restrictions-replacing-trumps-travel-ban/.

Office of the Press Secretary, "Statement by Secretary of Homeland Security John Kelly on President's Executive Order Signed Today,"

The Department of Homeland Security, March 6, 2017. https://www.dhs.gov/news/2017/03/06/statement-secretary-homeland-security-john-kelly-presidents-executive-order-signed.

Panduranga, Harsha, Faiza Patel, and Michael Price, "Extreme Vetting and the Muslim Ban," Brennan Center for Justice, October 2, 2017. https://www.brennancenter.org/publication/extreme-vetting-and-muslim-ban.

"Sanctuary Cities: Top 3 Pros and Cons," ProCon.org, Dec. 8, 2016. https://www.procon.org/headline.php?headlineID=005333.

Simons, George. "What Just Happened to the Travel Ban?," *SimpleCitizen*, October 2017. https://learn.simplecitizen.com/2017/10/just-happened-travel-ban/.

"Trump's Executive Order on Immigration, Annotated," NPR, January 31, 2017. https://www.npr.org/2017/01/31/512439121/trumps-executive-order-on-immigration-annotated.

Websites

Center for Security Policy (www.centerforsecuritypolicy.org)
The Center attempts to organize and direct public policy relating to US national security. The website offers publications such as articles, press releases, and transcripts from Center events.

The Department of Homeland Security (www.dhs.gov)
This government agency is responsible for securing the United States from threats, including terrorism. Learn about the agency and get press releases and fact sheets from the website.

Immigrant Solidarity Network (ISN) (www.immigrantsolidarity.org)
ISN works with leading immigrant rights, students, and labor groups to organize community immigrant rights education campaigns. The website offers links to resources such as knowing your rights at protests, student walkouts, and checkpoints.

Index

Picture Credits

Cover Danny Lehman/Corbis Documentary/Getty Images; p. 11 Hulton Archive/Getty Images; p. 14 Everett Historical/Shutterstock.com; p. 25 Christian Inton/RTR/Newscom; p. 31 John Moore/Getty Images; p. 37 Win McNamee/Getty Images; p. 43 a katz/Shutterstock.com; p. 45 © AP Images; p. 47 John Gomez/Shutterstock.com; p. 52 Jeff Greenberg/Universal Images Group/Getty Images; p. 58 Christian Petersen/Getty Images; p. 65 John Panella/Shutterstock.com; p. 70 AFP/Newscom; p. 76 Jerry Horbert/Shutterstock.com; p. 79 David McNew/AFP/Getty Images; p. 85 Unai Beroiz/Shutterstock.com; p. 90 Mark Wallheiser/Getty Images; p. 96 Rawpixel.com/Shutterstock.com; p. 101 The Boston Globe/Getty Images.